Ethics of an Artificial Person

LOST RESPONSIBILITY IN PROFESSIONS
AND ORGANIZATIONS

ETHICS OF AN ARTIFICIAL PERSON

Lost Responsibility in Professions and Organizations

Elizabeth Wolgast

Stanford University Press, Stanford, California   1992

Stanford University Press, Stanford, California
© 1992 by the Board of Trustees of the Leland Stanford Junior University
Printed in the United States of America

CIP data appear at the end of the book

For Dick Brown and other Berkeley Friends

Acknowledgments

A NUMBER OF WRITERS have been concerned about ethical problems in the professions and politics, and some excellent works address the morality of public servants and lawyers. Richard Wasserstrom, Thomas Nagel, David Luban, and William Simon belong at the top of my list of sources, and I have cited them freely. They pointed the way toward my argument, whose intent is to give the discussion greater generality and to bring illumination from the side of moral theory.

Other scholars helped guide my research and prod the argument along. I'm grateful to Linda Krieger, Col. Anthony Hartle, Carl Wellman, A. I. Melden, and Rita Manning for their discussions and comments on the manuscript or parts of it. I cannot imagine what this work would be without their help. David Skover, Neil MacCormick, Nicholas Rescher, and Laura Nader gave vital help with sources. A large debt is owed to the faculty who taught philosophy at the United States Military Academy while I was there, in the fall of 1987. Their help with sources and military examples, their lively and friendly skepticism, and their moral seriousness helped to anchor my argument and enrich my understanding. Johanna Wolgast gave the manuscript a thoughtful critical reading, while an anonymous reviewer for Stanford University Press and David Sabia led me to sources and gave helpful suggestions; I am thankful to all three. And Ellen F. Smith, who edited the manuscript for Stanford Press, was wonderful.

The National Endowment for the Humanities, an independent federal agency, supported the project with a fellowship,
and the Rockefeller Foundation granted a fellowship at their
Bellagio Center.

Part of the argument of Chapter 6 appeared in W. Maihofer
and G. Sprenger, eds., *Law and the State in Modern Times* (Stutt-
gart: Steiner Verlag, 1990).

E. W.

Contents

Ethics of an Artificial Person

LOST RESPONSIBILITY IN PROFESSIONS
AND ORGANIZATIONS

Introduction

ARTIFICIAL PERSONS speak and act in the name of others, can commit and obligate them. The idea comes from Thomas Hobbes, who also calls them "feigned" or "fictional" persons. By their standing in place of someone else whom they "personate," their actions *become* the actions of the other, Hobbes says. Hobbes introduces "artificial person" to explain how government represents citizens: government is the people's spokesman and acts in their collective name, but he points to other, more everyday examples: parents who decide for young children and servants sent on errands. Each acts in the name of someone else. In modern institutions there are many more examples: corporations acting for stockholders, lawyers, stockbrokers, real estate agents—the list is enormous. Yet the implications of this conception—especially moral ones—Hobbes leaves unexplored.

Using an agent to accomplish something has a long tradition in law, and we will trace some of that history. But while legal discussions of agency often focus on commercial agents, Hobbes's idea, being broad and philosophically developed, is relevant to many other contexts and provides a useful fulcrum for exploring their similarities. The most curious feature of the various forms of artificial persons is that actions are done by someone other than whoever *does* them in a physical sense. One challenge is therefore to understand what this means and how there can be such action.[1] I will focus on the moral aspect of

---

[1] In "Sending Someone Else," which first appeared in *Philosophical Investigations* 9, 2 (Apr. 1986) and was revised as chapter 4 of my *The Grammar of Justice*

these actions, particularly how responsibility for them can be located, for in this respect they contrast dramatically with actions without any intermediary.

Locating responsibility is unproblematic on Hobbes's account.[2] The sovereign is immune from criticism; his position as "personator" of the citizenry allows them no room for complaint or dissent. True, his function is to secure their persons and property from threats among themselves, but he has wide latitude in how to do this, and since his actions belong to the citizens, their criticism has no purchase, no basis. In modern contexts, however, artificial persons are not in the same way immune to criticism. Figures in important positions—notably politicians, lawyers, brokers, corporate executives, and military personnel—come under moral attack for things they do in the course of representing others. But the arrangement of artificial person gets in the way of clear assignments of responsibility— and partly for the reason Hobbes gives, namely that the thing done is done in the name of another. The details of this consequence and its ramifications for agency need to be explored.

My procedure is to begin by considering how artificial persons or agents are embedded in our institutions and professions and how they are there defined and conceived. Then I ask how such arrangements, with their rationale and paradigm, relate to morality with its paradigm of an autonomous and responsible person. The point is to lay professional and organizational arrangements against the measure of moral theory. When we do this, we discover a deep and intractable dissonance.

That dissonance is readily discernible in a wide variety of positions. Thus the advantage of dealing with artificial persons is to give the issues a larger conceptual framework, making it unnecessary to limit ourselves to the particularities of any one form and allowing us to see particular problems under a large theoretical light. Hobbes's idea, abstract as it is, vitiates the compart-

---

(Ithaca, N.Y.: Cornell University Press, 1987), I argued that the virtue of a virtuous action changes when it is done by a representative; its virtue is not conserved. The present essay argues that responsibility is also not conserved in such arrangements.

[2] Modern writers have also seemed uninterested in the moral side of representation; for instance, Hanna Pitkin, *The Concept of Representation* (Berkeley: University of California Press, 1967) and A. H. Birch, *Representation* (New York: Praeger, 1971).

mentalization of problems and the limitations of special background assumptions. We freely cross disciplinary boundaries, as well as the line between theory and practice, and allow practices to cast their light back on the theory and show us its deficiencies. In short, this approach reorients many of the much-discussed issues of professional, business, and military ethics and reveals them as variations on one deeply rooted theme.

The important question that evolves from this is whether institutional practice can have priority over moral claims, and here I have brought to bear some practices of other cultures and their distinct institutions. This is to say that I do not treat our institutions in their current forms as final and unalterable. On the contrary, I assume that if such arrangements frustrate moral evaluation, that is an argument for change. But before proposing changes, we need to have in clear view the reasoning that entrenches these problems in social thinking and fixes the form of institutions with their practices which are then resistant to change. I will argue that the often-made recommendation to address the issues by means of instituting or revising codes of conduct leaves this underlying reasoning in place and thus furthers the disguising and hiding of morally troublesome practices by innocent descriptions.

A note on the context of my discussion is in order. Although the concepts we explore apply very generally, the context in which criticisms are made and examples drawn is that of U.S. institutions. Proposals for change are also cast in terms familiar to Americans, and occasionally Western cultures, yet their implications for other cultures are clear in the background. The moral theory invoked is also Western and, as I argue, necessarily *ours*. We have no more abstract base to view things from, nor does it make sense to want one. Thus, part of my approach is to engage argument with examples so that the examples illuminate the theory, not merely confirm it. This means that practices and concepts are doubly related, mutually reflecting on the soundness of one another. In our daily lives we make unequivocal judgments about examples; at the same time we hold firmly to certain moral ideas. Where our convictions regarding these two are revealed as dissonant, we have confusion about both what to say and what to do. Thus my effort is directed toward understanding as thoroughly as possible the relation between practice and concept with regard to artificial persons and toward probing the points of dissonance.

Among the prominent forms of artificial person are the military, political representatives, lawyers, bureaucracies, and corporations: these provide my examples. Some unique problems of government and corporations are discussed in separate chapters, but the central thesis applies to all of them.

Besides serving to discourage the treatment of moral problems in terms of specialized codes or institutional obligations, this approach discourages us from seeing moral issues in terms of an individual who, perhaps tragically, must choose between larger and smaller evils. My argument is that contexts are important, not only as they affect the significance of actions, but as they influence the more fundamental idea of what a person is. Thus institutions themselves become part of the picture of actions occurring in them; they affect and constrain the actions in many ways. The upshot is that if we are to redeem the attribution of personal responsibility, our institutions may need reshaping.

To locate the roots of the moral problems, I examine artificial persons from different sides. I view them as roles, with the implications that go with that terminology. I look at them from the side of moral theory with its central paradigm, the autonomous individual. I consider artificial persons as instruments, a great variety of them, who have great usefulness. Finally, I consider the way this familiar arrangement bears on what it means, practically and morally, to be a person. This multifaceted treatment shows familiar and intractable issues under changing lights, illuminates them from the inside. It allows them to develop their full depth as issues for moral philosophy and at the same time brings the need for change into high relief.

Hobbes's notion lends itself to this purpose by embracing various professions and positions known for their moral hazards. It helps us to see how artificial persons generate distinctive moral issues and create moral conflicts that traditional moral theory is helpless to resolve. It allows us to map the points of moral tension between various professions and moral theory.

We appear bound by a long-standing tradition, and a pragmatic commitment to speed and economy, to use such agents;

thus we easily fall in with the seductive language of roles that supports such use. But despite their neutral description, these practices are not morally neutral; rather they affect the lives and thinking of those who participate in them in ways that are morally unsalutory; and finally, they give their own shape to what we mean by a morally competent person. An implication of such interconnection is that individual moral responsibility and the capacity for moral action are not fixed features of human life; they do not remain unaffected by institutional structure but require contextual conditions that are fragile and susceptible to changes of context. A critical examination of such contexts is therefore profoundly important.

Given the conflict between the features of institutions and the requirements of morality, one might imagine that, instead of attacking our present institutions, we could redefine the moral paradigms to fit the social world we have, the world that traditional moral ideas are at odds with. Could such conceptual changes relieve the problems at the theoretical level and simply leave the practices intact? I argue that they could not, that this proposal contains a conceptual error. Failing this remedy, my conclusion is that to bring institutions into line with moral theory will require enormous rethinking and institutional restructuring. The alternative is to resign ourselves to the loss in many contexts of a usable idea of responsibility.

The legal tradition of agency to which Hobbes's idea belongs is traced in Chapter 1. The earliest paradigm of such arrangements is the identification of slaves, servants, and family members with the master of the house: their actions and commitments are attributed to him. This model casts a long shadow over many later, sophisticated commercial practices and introduces paradoxical moral implications.

Chapter 2 traces how responsibility loses coherence in artificial-person contexts. It reviews how professional practices are defended, and asks if they can be adjusted so as to allow for moral revision. Current discussions of professional ethics tend to be framed in terms of *role* moralities, separating a person's character from her role. I argue that this move is hazardous for any coherent idea of individual responsibility.

Artificial persons occupy roles; thus the language of roles seems natural for discussing them. In Chapter 3, therefore, I look at roles in a large variety—king, wife, actor, waiter—and ask what having such roles implies. Can they be put on and taken off without affecting the holder's identity? Are they morally neutral? Even for specific cases the answers are surprisingly difficult. This sets the stage for my claim that looking at professional and work activities in terms of roles gives little purchase on misdeeds done in them; instead it helps to screen them from moral criticism. In part, this results from the theatrical model, which suggests that a person and her role are distinct and metaphysically separated. I conclude that considering agents in terms of roles is problematic, that an alternative account is needed.

How can an action be done by one person in someone else's name? Chapter 4 looks at artificial persons in terms of the moral paradigm, most clearly delineated by Kant, in which a person is responsible for knowingly and voluntarily deciding on and then doing whatever she does. It is the paradigm of autonomous action. In its light the artificial person's actions are inherently paradoxical, for it makes attributing one person's actions to someone else impossible.

Some artificial persons are compound agents like committees, boards, councils, and corporations. These are discussed in Chapter 5. Being multiple, these artificial persons are even more peculiar than others. Some of the problems are common to all compound agents, but corporations have the further peculiarity that they are accorded the legal status of persons. This needs discussion. I argue that the "personhood" of corporations helps to obscure rather than locate responsibility for corporate actions.

Although modern democratic theory derives from Hobbes, it transforms Hobbes's giant into a domestic servant. As a docile artificial person, we ask, can government be held morally accountable? Chapter 6 argues that it cannot, and it cannot for the same reason that responsibility is problematic for other artificial persons. The implication is that political representation needs a radically different account and understanding from what is usually given.

Agents and artificial persons are often used as instruments by someone else; thus Chapter 7 subjects the use of people as instruments to moral scrutiny. Although such positions are widely and casually accepted, this impersonal use of people is morally

demeaning, I argue. Thus the moral acceptability of such practices needs to be considered despite their ubiquitous presence
and their apparent indispensability.

Chapter 8 deals with the tension between the idea of a person
and the institutional arrangements of agency. It argues that a
person, morally speaking, requires a certain kind of social setting, one that gives meaning and scope for moral actions. The
meaning of being a person thus changes with the social contexts
in which people are set, which means that our institutions affect
our idea of humans in morally relevant ways.

Finally, Chapter 9 points to some directions for making
changes. If responsibility is to be a palpable feature of communal
life, then our institutions and professions need reshaping in
radical ways. To see what this means, we call on other cultures
in order to see our own at an imaginative distance and to show
our institutions as options within a spectrum of possibilities.
The practical problems of a reshaping are formidable, that is
granted. But the situation that our institutions force upon us is
morally problematic in an extreme degree. The benefit of a theoretical understanding is a clear view of the choices we weigh.

ONE

Feigned and Fictional Persons

Qui facit per alium facit per se. [Who acts through another acts himself.]
Latin saying

It is just as possible to bring wrongs to pass through free human agents as through slaves, animals, or natural forces.
Oliver Wendell Holmes, Jr., "Agency I"

A PERSON "is he whose words or actions are considered, either as his own, or as representing the words or actions of an other man, or of any other thing to whom they are attributed," Hobbes says. Two possibilities are open: one can act either in one's own name, as a "natural person," or in the name of someone else; and "when [someone's actions] are considered as representing the words and actions of an other, then is he a Feigned or Artificiall Person."[1]

"Person," Hobbes observes, derives from the Latin *persona*, which means a disguise or appearance on the stage. "So that a Person, is the same that an Actor is, both on the Stage and in common Conversation; and to Personate, is to Act, or Represent himselfe, or an other; and he that acteth another, is said to beare his Person, or act in his name." Since "person" is connected with a theatrical context, Hobbes likens the way that an actor on stage portrays some character to the way an artificial person acts as someone else. The objection leaps to mind that while an actor

---

[1] Hobbes, *Leviathan* (Hammondsworth, Eng.: Penguin, 1961), I: 16, 217. Like Hobbes, I don't distinguish between agents and representatives. Such a distinction is made by Hanna Pitkin, who says an agent is someone who "does the actual work. . . . When we call a man someone's agent we are saying that he is the tool or instrument by which the other acts. . . . When we call him a representative . . . we are saying . . . that the entire corporation is present in him"; *The Concept of Representation* (Berkeley: University of California Press, 1967), 125. Underlying her distinction are differences in people's importance and exercise of discretion: some employees have too little power to represent; instead they are tools or instruments; 124–25. I treat these as differences of degree.

can play a part, no one in real circumstances can act *as* another person. It seems inherently strange to suppose that one person can be fully responsible for what another does. Hobbes does require that where a capable adult is represented, an agreement is necessary and the scope of the authority must be specified. But under these conditions the author is responsible for his agent's actions, effective or futile, right or wrong, and regardless of whether they were expressly ordered: "their words and actions [are] Owned by those whom they represent." One person does something, the other gets credited with it. "The Person is the Actor; and he that owneth his words and actions, is the Author."[2]

Hobbes's idea is large and metaphorical; and since artificial persons take different forms, their differences must be kept in mind.[3] For instance, while citizens are responsible for the actions of their governments, infants and the insane are not responsible for their representatives in the same way. In fact, it is precisely children's inability to act as responsible adults that requires someone to act for them. Sometimes, Hobbes says, a person "may be Personated . . . but can be no Author," as with a child or an incompetent who can do many things *only* through representatives. But human persons are generally able to act for themselves, and thus are the authors of what their representatives do; in sum, the author *does* it. That means that a representative who makes a "covenant by Authority . . . bindeth thereby the Author, no lesse than if he [the author] had made it himselfe; and no lesse subjecteth him to all the consequences of the same."[4]

---

[2]*Leviathan* I: 16, 217. There is some difficulty in Hobbes's account here, since he first attributes an artificial person's action to *him* and then to the author. This ambiguity seems linguistic but is inherent in the arrangement, as we shall see.

[3]Some writers—e.g., John Rawls (*A Theory of Justice* [Cambridge, Mass.; Harvard University Press, 1971]) and Peter French (*Collective and Corporate Responsibility* [New York: Columbia University Press, 1984])—neglect this. They speak as if only a legal corporation is a "fictional person." While Hobbes's term includes corporations, this application is not central or guiding in his theory. Harold Reuschlein and William Gregory's handbook on legal agency makes another confusion—e.g., "corporations are said to be 'artificial persons.' As such, they can act only through agents"; *Agency and Partnership* (St. Paul, Minn.: West Publishing Co., 1978), 5. In Hobbes's meaning, agents *are* artificial persons usually. These authors also seem to confuse Hobbes's idea with the legal idea that corporations are "fictional persons."

[4]*Leviathan* I: 16, 217. Hobbes's conception is broader than legal agency. For instance Reuschlein and Gregory emphasize the control a principal (author) has

There are many interesting cases where nonhumans are spoken for by artificial persons: a church, a hospital, even a bridge may be personated, Hobbes says. And "the true God may be Personated" by his particular spokesmen.[5] And in politics "a multitude of men, are made *One* Person, when they are by one man, or one Person, Represented; so that it be done with the consent of every one of that Multitude in particular. For it is the *Unity* of the Representer, not the *Unity* of the Represented, that maketh the Person *One*."[6] A representative makes a group of people into one person.

Yet when it comes to responsibility, the multitude remain many. The citizens "cannot be understood for one; but many Authors, of every thing their Representative . . . doth in their name; Every man giving their common Representer, Authority from himselfe . . . and owning all the actions the Representer doth." What the representative does, the citizens do through him, its action is theirs as individuals, and they are unequivocally responsible. This multiplicity of authors must be dealt with whenever a group of people designate someone to speak for them, for members may differ in their choice of a representative and in what they want her to do. How can this be settled, and how can unity be attained? "The voyce of the greater number, must be considered as the voyce of them all," says Hobbes; it is "the only voyce the Representative hath." Lacking a better means, a majority is employed to make the many voices into one.[7]

---

over his agent. They explain that this is why insane people cannot have agents, yet they *can* be represented by a Hobbesian artificial person. While similar reasoning would show that babies cannot have legal agents, Reuschlein and Gregory report that "an infant can make contracts for necessaries and perform necessary duties [and] . . . an infant is liable in tort for tortious acts which he has directed"; *Agency and Partnership*, 21–22. The legal conception of agent thus apparently lacks some of the clarity of "artificial person."

[5] Moses and Jesus were such spokesmen. Hobbes doesn't say whether a priest or minister acts as God when performing some ceremonial functions, e.g., marriages. However it seems unlikely Hobbes would say that a priest can *commit* God to anything. John Chipman Gray writes that "in theology it may be that the chief artificial person is the Church," but here he is thinking of the Church in analogy with a corporation, which is not Hobbes's point; *The Nature and Sources of the Law*, 2nd ed. (New York: Macmillan, 1931), 65.

[6] *Leviathan* I: 16, 220.

[7] Ibid., 220–21. Interestingly, the majority principle plays no part in setting up Hobbes's state or in determining its policies. *Everyone* must be party to the original pact; but after the sovereign is instated, the citizen-authors have no role to play in deciding policy.

I

Acting through a representative is a practice common and accepted in contemporary life. Legal theorist John Chipman Gray says that "normal human beings . . . can exercise their rights through agents, such as servants, bailiffs, or attorneys, and they can delegate to their agents the decision of the question whether the rights of the principles shall be exercised or not."[8] An agent can exercise a person's rights for him, and in this, as in many things, it is largely a matter of how one wants to accomplish something—in person or by using another.

One common kind of representative is an attorney. Gerald Postema describes a lawyer's function this way.

The characteristic activities of lawyers often require the lawyer to act in the place of the client . . . [using] his capacities to deliberate, reason, argue, and act in the public arena. . . . The lawyer . . . acts as the client's *agent*. . . . He often acts, speaks, and argues in the place of the client. He enters into relationships with others in the name of the client. When he argues in his client's behalf, he often presents his client's argument; when he acts, he is often said to be "exercising his client's rights" and what he does is typically attributable to the client. Thus . . . the lawyer becomes an extension of the legal, and to an extent the moral, personality of the client.[9]

One hears plainly the echoes of Hobbes.

The practice of doing something through an agent has a long history. It is found in Roman times, where a master is held responsible for all actions of his slave or servant.[10] The foundation for the practice, Oliver Wendell Holmes, Jr. says, is the identification of the head of a household with its members, whose actions, like their possessions, became the master's. "As all family rights and obligations were simply attributes of the *persona* of the family head," any economic transaction of theirs involved him. "For that purpose they were one with the *paterfamilias*." On a similar basis "early [English] law dealt with married women on

[8] Gray, *Nature and Sources of the Law*, 29.
[9] Gerald Postema, "Moral Responsibility in Professional Ethics," *New York University Law Review* 55, 1 (Apr. 1980): 76–77.
[10] The Greeks also used representatives for commercial transactions, but not so widely as the Romans. For instance, they made slaves individually accountable and punishable for their misdeeds, and they attributed a slave's action to a master only where the slave acted on express orders; see J. Walter Jones, *The Law and Legal Theory of the Greeks* (London: Oxford University Press, 1956), 278, 283.

the footing of servants." So if a woman was party to some transaction prior to marriage, after marriage her husband simply took
her place: "in theory of law there was no transfer, because the
stranger [the husband] had become the same person as the con-
tractee." By the same reasoning free agents in the household,
including guests, were also identified with the master. The head
of the house thus "personates" a variety of other people, and in
this process "two [or more] persons were feigned to be one." The
basic paradigm or fiction is "that within the scope of the agency,
principal and agent are one," as Holmes writes. This means that
heads of households can be held legally responsible for actions
they haven't expressly commanded, and even for actions
"which they not only have not authorized but have forbid-
den."[11]

Hobbes drew on this tradition and contributed to it with his
conception of artificial person.[12] But despite the common use of
agents, identifying an agent with her author raises nagging concerns—not only because, as Holmes charges, it fosters bad law
and doctrinal confusion, but because it brings moral confusion.
Does acting through an agent change the moral quality of what
is done? How can responsibility for such deeds be allocated?
These are questions I will explore. Their answers promise to cast
light on contemporary questions about political and professional immorality, a cloudiness that affects many contexts of our
lives.

II

Since a servant acts for his master, the doctrine of agency dictates that "the master must pay for the act if it is wrongful and
has the advantage of it if it is right." Although the language is
familiar and seems unexceptionable, Holmes worries nonethe-

[11] Oliver Wendell Holmes, Jr., "Agency I," in Holmes, *Collected Legal Papers*
(New York: Harcourt Brace & Co., 1920), 58, 61, 73, 49. Holmes adds that the
tendency to identify acts of guests with those of their host persists to modern
times. Wives' actions were also sometimes attributed to their husbands, Holmes
notes; 61. Also see A. S. Diamond, *Primitive Law* (London: Watts, 1935) 308–13.
For modern justifications for thinking of a household as one person, see my
Equality and the Rights of Women (Ithaca, N.Y.: Cornell University Press, 1980),
ch. 6.

[12] Holmes readily acknowledges Hobbes's contribution to the doctrine of identification; "Agency II," 83n.

less that "the mere habit of using these phrases . . . makes it likely that other cases will be brought within the penumbra of the same thought on no more substantial ground than the way of thinking which the words have brought about." The more we practice the substitution of one person for another, the more natural the practice becomes. And the variety of artificial persons becomes greater as the patriarchal metaphor hardens into common speech. A sheriff and his undersheriff become "one officer"; an employer becomes responsible for actions of employees who are neither servants nor slaves.[13] And military actions are seen as the deeds of the citizens in whose name they are done, whether these authors command them or not.

Moral concern over what is done in someone else's name takes various forms. Citizens worry about what their government and military do, and, true to Hobbes's account, they see themselves as the authors—sometimes of terrible and censurable deeds. One writer remarks that "it is an important fact, a *personal* fact, about the people [who objected to the Vietnam war] that they were citizens of a nation guilty of war crimes" and felt personally ashamed of actions they neither committed nor commanded.[14]

The root metaphor for agency, echoed in Hobbes's giant who rules impetuous citizens, is the figure of master and slave. That case is the easiest for identifying two people as one, because legally the slave lacks an identity; he may be considered nonhuman, or human only with qualifications.[15] Thus, whatever he does must be attributed to someone else, and to whom more sensibly than his master? It is like charging a father with the offenses of his child, and ancient Greeks thought these relations analogous. A master must be protector of his slaves as he was of his children. But the farther one gets from the slave case the less

[13] Ibid., 59, 79.

[14] Gerald Postema, "Self-Image, Integrity, and Professional Responsibility," in David Luban, ed., *The Good Lawyer* (Totowa, N.J.: Rowman & Allanheld, 1984), 300.

[15] For a discussion of the view that slaves are less than human, see Stanley Cavell, *The Claim of Reason* (New York: Oxford University Press, 1979), 372–78. Accounts on this theme go back to Aristotle, who thought that both women and slaves were by nature inferior to free male citizens. On the other hand J. Walter Jones observes that in Athens slaves might own considerable property, and that "bankers were not infrequently slaves"; *Law and Legal Theory of the Greeks*, 283. Athenian slaves also had some rights to bring legal proceedings.

plausible it is to identify two people as one. For instance, a servant is something like a slave, and thus his master "never can shelter himself from punishment by laying the blame on his agent," one jurist wrote, because "the wrong done by the servant is looked upon in law as the wrong of the master himself." Yet common sense says that an agent who acts without being specifically commanded must bear *some* responsibility. And while agency doctrine didn't support suing a servant *in his capacity as servant*, it came to allow that a servant "cannot rid himself of his responsibility as a freeman, and may be sued as a free wrong-doer."[16]

Here the theory whose principal virtue was simplicity leads into tangles. How, with regard to a single action, can master and servant be identified in some respects but not altogether? What kind of identification is both legally strict and qualified?

III

The use of artificial persons sometimes seems necessary, as with incompetents or children who cannot act or make commitments by themselves.[17] With children and incompetents there is no author in the usual sense; still, someone does something in someone else's name. Thus, this kind of authorless action seems curious even for Hobbes. Yet some legal writings treat such representation as commonplace. For instance, A. Phillips Griffiths explains the practice of representing

dead men, the totally paralyzed, some lunatics, and corporations . . . [because] it is a necessary condition of the application of the concept of a person that the object to which it is applied should be thought of as capable of action. . . . At some point there must be persons who can act without being represented in turn . . . and this is in general true only of individual human beings.[18]

[16]Holmes, "Agency I," 77–78 (quoting Blackstone), 79. One needs to keep in mind that the tradition of legal agency was a developing and changing one, in its view of employees and servants as well as in other respects.

[17]The difference between "artificial person" and "agent" in the legal sense can be seen in the instances of incompetents and children. Reuschlein and Gregory insist on the need for consent, which eliminates slaves, young children, and incompetents from having agents; *Agency and Partnership*, 3.

[18]A. Phillips Griffiths, "How Can One Person Represent Another?," *Aristotelian Society Supplement* 34 (1960). Some would deny that the dead are representable; for example, Gray, *Nature and Sources of the Law*, 38–39. Yet he is willing to

Since paralyzed people are persons and since a person can act, they must be able to act somehow; therefore they need someone to act for them. That is his reasoning, but it lacks consistency. Paralyzed persons need representatives because *they cannot act*. So one should conclude according to the definition that *they are not persons*. Saying, as Griffiths does, that they must be able to act anyway because they *are* persons, belies the reason for their *having* a representative, which is that they can't act! It would be more sensible to say that some persons can act and others can't, and that an able person can *assist* someone who can't act herself. One would then treat responsibility for acting in behalf of someone else in a special way, using special conceptions, rather than assimilate it to the case of an able-bodied person acting for herself.[19]

Legal theory is a realm of strange maneuvers, particularly in this area of babies and incompetent persons. John Chipman Gray says that the term "person" is restricted to creatures who have will. Yet, he continues, "some human beings have no wills; such are babies and the insane," and without wills they cannot do anything. How can we make a theoretical adjustment and preserve the human status of babies? "Though without wills, new-born babies and idiots have rights," and having rights they must be persons, he argues.[20] This tolerance of oddities appears in the law's inference that newborn babies are persons *because* they have rights. Nevertheless, such persons "act" without understanding or even recognizing what they do, act as puppets do, only by metaphor.[21]

give rights to fetuses, animals, and even supernatural beings; 40. Unmarried women in Roman times were also such quasi persons, needing a representative. Diamond writes that the law "placed and kept unmarried women under perpetual tutory, and the authority of her guardian and trustee was necessary to give legal validity to her acts"; *Primitive Law*, 268.

[19] One way around this problem is to make a distinction between human beings and persons, as does Hans Kelsen, who says "the physical person is a human being, whereas the juristic person is not. . . . Man is a concept of biology and physiology. . . . Person is a concept of jurisprudence"; *General Theory of Law and State*, trans. Anders Wedberg (New York: Russell & Russell, 1961), 94. This accords with John Locke's claim that "person" is a forensic concept applying only to creatures subject to law.

[20] Gray, *Nature and Sources of the Law*, 29.

[21] There is a big difference between a handicapped person who acts despite a disability and one for whom another person acts. An instance of the former is physicist Stephen Hawking who "speaks" through a computerized system.

Again a common-sense view is that when an incapacitated or incompetent person cannot take care of her affairs, she needs someone to take care of them or to help her to do so. Describing such an arrangement by saying that one person acts *through* another, as if the latter were a mechanical device, is contrived. It distorts the situation humanly speaking. And moral difficulties follow in its wake.

A similar problem concerns government, which is grounded in the inability of citizens to speak and act as a nation. Like a lunatic or a baby, a community cannot speak for itself. It needs a government; thus, so long as he rules, the sovereign fulfills his crucial function, which is to give the citizens a single voice. The Hobbesian citizens thus have the worst of both worlds: they are treated like incompetent children but are fully responsible for whatever government does.[22]

IV

Most of a person's practical needs for a professional, such as a doctor, do not involve a transfer of power or identifying oneself with the professional. Nor do such relations usually involve immunity from responsibility and moral criticism, as Hobbes claims for the sovereign. On the contrary, a doctor acting for an incompetent or unconscious patient takes on a heavy responsibility, the heavier *because* the patient's needs, like a child's, are so great. Following this line, Hobbes *might* have said that the sovereign's responsibility is like that of a parent to his children, or a shepherd to his flock, or a captain to his crew. It is among the heaviest moral burdens that exist and may require great selflessness.[23]

Hobbes's picture of human nature blocks this inference, however, for his is a picture where people act without concern for anyone but themselves and are unable to put their interests

---

Hawking is clearly the agent who speaks, despite his dependence on technology. Bringing in a representative to act and speak for him is altogether different.

[22] Hobbes appears inconsistent about the government as an artificial person. If the people cannot speak without a government, then, like infants, they should be exempt from authorship, not fully and unequivocally responsible.

[23] Such a paternalistic view of sovereignty and of government in general was onerous to both Hobbes and Locke, particularly as it was often linked with the claim that the sovereign is superior to his subjects.

aside for any reason. Thus, while citizens are busy pursuing their private desires, the sovereign is doubly a natural person. He acts as himself, as well as for others, and he acts without a framework of constraints.

The legal tradition of artificial persons is guided by a certain gestalt, the linked figures of master and slave or servant, respectively models of power and powerlessness. But how can such a model apply to modern relations between fully competent and equal humans, professionals and their clients, government and the citizens? How does it harmonize with our moral tradition? The moral difficulties of the slave-and-master relation are plain enough, but the interpretation of these difficulties in modern descendents of that relation is not similarly clear. They need to be ferreted out and addressed.

Who Is Responsible?

*In virtue of my membership in some larger whole or wholes, how can I
reasonably be expected to take responsibility for what these bodies do in circumstances where I could have no conceivable influence on their actions?*
W. H. Walsh, "Pride, Shame, and Responsibility"

IN THEIR VARIOUS forms, artificial persons make decisions
that commit other people. At the same time, the power to speak
and act for another makes responsibility problematic, for common sense wants to ask who *really* did what was done, who is
responsible. The answer is difficult to find.

I

Lawyers provide a clear case of the difficulty, and from both
within and without the legal profession is the focus of much
moral criticism. The reason is this: a lawyer's position requires
him to act, but to act not as himself or for his own purposes and
sometimes not on his own judgment. The cause he pleads—
even eloquently and passionately—and may appear to endorse
is not his, and his expressions of indignation and sympathy, his
praise of his client and expressions of scorn for the opposing
client are also not personally his. Thus, to the problems that apply to other artificial persons is added a large component of dissembling.

It is clear why responsibility for actions that a lawyer undertakes for a client should be ambiguous. It is not the client who
does what is done, but the lawyer. However, since the lawyer acts
on behalf of and in the name of his client, the action isn't strictly
his either. The responsibility must then be the client's; he is the
one who brings suit, who wins or loses, and who may pay the

judgment or even go to jail. We go back and forth—the lawyer acts for the client, not himself; the client is detached but stands to benefit or suffer.

A lawyer's immunity from criticism is defended in this way by one writer:

> We must distinguish between what lawyers do and what clients do *through their lawyers*. . . . The content of a lawyer's action, focused by intentions solely on the legal lever-pulling, may be entirely unproblematic, morally speaking, although what the client seeks to do through the actions of the lawyer may well be morally problematic. And . . . since all that one must take responsibility for are one's own actions and their (intended) consequences, there is no bad faith in refusing to face aspects of professional activity that are not properly attributable to one's own agency.[1]

On this account the lawyer simply performs suitable legal moves; she isn't responsible for the ends that guide them. She serves as an instrument of someone else, and her standards are those of competent lawyers—of knowing how to use legal rules and practices for a client's advantage. She files papers, prepares forms, sends letters to appropriate officers; she gives persuasive argument in or out of court and in general displays the knowledge and skills she is trained in. At the conclusion she is paid.

But then the question arises: what difference is there between a lawyer and a county clerk whose job is to fill out forms, say, or a bookkeeper who balances books, or a pharmacist who fills a prescription?[2] The clerk may assist in a dispossession, the books may contain evidence of mismanagement, the prescription may cause harm. Like lawyers, they do as they are trained and fill their positions; but unlike lawyers, they don't suffer moral criticism. If they aren't responsible for the consequences they bring about in their work, why should lawyers be?

Indeed, according to the American Bar Association code, a lawyer is not culpable in her pursuit of a client's interests so long as no law is violated.[3] She is no more responsible for her client's

---

[1] Gerald Postema, "Self-Image, Integrity, and Professional Responsibility," in David Luban, ed., *The Good Lawyer* (Totowa, N.J.: Rowman & Allanheld, 1984), 302.

[2] I mean company employees here, not Certified Public Accountants, who are supposed to be representatives of the public and therefore artificial persons with the same vulnerability to criticism as lawyers.

[3] Also see Murray Schwartz, who reports as the "common understanding" that "when acting as an advocate, a lawyer is neither legally, professionally, nor

purposes than a pharmacist is for a physician's diagnosis. One hesitates to accept this argument, because lawyers generally know quite well what is behind the actions they are involved in; they are unlike most clerks and pharmacists, who may not be privy to the whole purpose and plan, who see only their detached contributions. Thus the lawyer's defense would be strengthened if it had the additional stipulation that she doesn't know what the likely effects of her actions will be. Then her excuse would fairly resemble that of clerks, accountants, and pharmacists: we only do what we are told. A lawyer would say, "I had no idea why I was bringing this suit or what would happen as a result." Or if she were incompetent or deceived by her client, we would sympathize with her: "Poor person, she was *used"*—without her understanding or consent.

However, the lawyer's nonaccountability can't depend on ignorance or incompetence; lawyers take pride in knowing how they can be most helpful, claim to know better than clients how to achieve their ends, and are pleased to lend their talents and skills to be maximally helpful. Single-mindedness in helping the client is a professional virtue, the English jurist Lord Brougham writes: "an advocate, in the discharge of his duty, knows but one person in all the world, and that person is his client. To save that client by all means and expedients, and at all hazards and costs to other persons, and, among them, to himself, is his first and only duty."[4]

II

Moral questions about the legal profession—and their answers—are often cast in terms of roles. Thus Richard Wasserstrom, himself a lawyer, is concerned with how an action done in a professional role can be "morally different from what it would have been if the role were not in the picture." "Appeal to

---

morally accountable for the means used or the ends achieved"; "The Professionalism and Accountability of Lawyers," *California Law Review* 66 (1978): 669.

[4] Lord Brougham, *The Trial of Queen Caroline* (1821); quoted in Charles Fried, *Right and Wrong* (Cambridge, Mass.: Harvard University Press, 1978), 177. The English jurist Henry Rolle is more daring and holds that "an attorney maliciously acting in a case" is not responsible if he does it "in the way of his calling and profession"; from Oliver Wendell Holmes, Jr., "Agency I," in Holmes, *Collected Legal Papers* (New York: Harcourt Brace & Co., 1920), 79.

the . . . role becomes a central part of the reasoning about the right thing to do"; this is shown by the way certain roles justify partiality. Thus a parent *should* be partial to the interests of her child, simply because she is a parent; the general should be more concerned about his own troops than the enemy's; and "it is thought to be . . . permissible and probably obligatory, once the lawyer has entered into the role of . . . lawyer for some client, . . . to do any number of things that otherwise might very well be morally criticizable." But this power of roles makes Wasserstrom uneasy: "the problem . . . is that behavior that is potentially criticizable on moral grounds is blocked from such criticism by an appeal to the existence of the actor's role. . . . Appeal to the . . . role seems to distort, limit, or make irrelevant what might otherwise be morally relevant."[5]

Appealing to roles is attractive, Wasserstrom thinks, "because roles provide a degree of moral simplification that makes it much easier to determine what one ought to do. . . . Psychologically, roles give a great power and security because they make moral life much simpler, less complex, and less vexing than it would be without them."[6] The demands of a role answer questions—which might otherwise be difficult—about what to do in given circumstances.

If one views the moral hazards of a professional in a framework of roles, it is understandable why those hazards are often addressed in terms of professional codes of ethics. The assumption is that if the code is tightened and the professional community made more aware, ethical problems can be corrected without altering the overall shape of the profession.[7] Of course, by suggesting that any moral problem can be answered by adjustments in role requirements, this approach works against radical change, against a deeper examination of what morality means. The shape of the profession is allowed to remain intact. Col. An-

---

[5] Richard Wasserstrom, "Roles and Morality," in Luban, ed., *The Good Lawyer*, 26–27, 28.

[6] Ibid., 29.

[7] For example, Richard de George suggests that the process of formulating a code for the military is a useful exercise in itself. It "forces a number of people within the military to think through in a fresh way their mission and the important obligations they as a group and as individuals have with respect to society as a whole. . . . Once adopted the code could generate continuing discussion and possible modification"; "Defining Moral Obligations: The Need for a Military Code of Ethics," *Army*, Dec. 1984, 30.

thony Hartle says of the military, for example, that "examining professional ethics in terms of role differentiation seems to be a reasonable way to reveal the moral structure within which military professionals work." He finds nothing problematic about the idea of a code that "consists of a set of rules and standards governing the conduct of members of a professional group."[8] The military code determines what they should do as members of the military.

Concerned with the gravity of many military decisions, Gen. Maxwell Taylor noted the absence of an explicit *ethical* code for the military and proposed that each officer should work one out on his own. He might begin with the idea that "an ideal officer is one who can be relied upon to carry out all assigned tasks and missions and, in doing so, get the most from his available resources with minimum loss and waste." Such an ideal person "would be deeply convinced of the importance of the military profession and its role, . . . [and] view himself as a descendant of the warrior, who, in company with the king, the priest, and the judge," has helped civilization survive. In the end Taylor believes that professional requirements must condition the moral ones and not the reverse.[9]

This is, of course, the central issue. Richard de George argues the other side, promoting the preeminence of moral understanding. The point of an ethical code is to raise the profession's standard above what is normally demanded: "Any profession . . . is appropriately given respect and autonomy only if it lives up to a higher moral code than is applicable to all." In particular this applies to the military, because "society places in [its hands] a monopoly on the use of the major instruments of force." Society's trust is consequently "enormous, and the corresponding burden on those who assume the trust and have custody of the monopoly of force is likewise enormous," he argues. But in view

---

[8] Anthony Hartle, *Moral Issues in Military Decision Making* (Lawrence: University Press of Kansas, 1989) 23, 24.

[9] Maxwell Taylor, "A Do-It-Yourself Professional Code for the Military," *Parameters: Journal of the U.S. Army War College* 10, 4 (Dec. 1980): 11. Most of Taylor's proposal concerns matters of leadership and discipline. And where these conflict with what one thinks is right? "As for his attitude toward the voice of conscience as a guide to military behavior, [the ideal officer] has serious doubts. . . . There are skeptics who maintain that it is little more than the voice of conventional morality, of ingrained habit." He also quotes H. L. Mencken: "Conscience is the inner voice that warns us that somebody may be looking"; 14.

of that trust, there should be a commitment to peacefulness and a cultivation of restraint in the use of that force.[10] This brings out the potential for conflict between a code and the basic military duties to obey and respect authority, duties of one piece in a large organizational machine.

A professional code, then, is a way of capturing the sum of duties of someone in that profession. But the question of where morality fits in remains. Gerald Postema wonders "whether, given the need for . . . a [professional] code, it is possible to preserve one's sense of responsibility" when professional responsibilities are detached from ordinary moral ones. His answer is no: "I contend that a sense of responsibility and sound practical judgment depend not only on the quality of one's professional training, but also on one's ability to draw on the resources of a broader moral experience . . . [which] in turn, requires that one seek to achieve a fully integrated moral personality."[11] Unless a person integrates his professional and nonprofessional life, he cannot fully satisfy his professional role, cannot be a good lawyer, Postema argues. This means that a code's claim to *morally* simplify a person's life is spurious.

Using the code as a guide or formula for making moral decisions may be simplifying, when as Wasserstrom says, roles and their obligations are substituted for decisions that demand the balancing of competing moral claims, a balancing that may be complex and difficult.[12] Role obligations and role moralities may thus contribute to simplicity in decision making *if* they exclude ordinary moral considerations—but in that case they add to the moral obscurity and complexity of whatever is done. The question is whether we should grant them this power to exclude.

III

Emile Durkheim argues, in support of role-defined moralities, that they are inevitable and morally beneficial. He uses the term "role" broadly. "The morals of a man are not those of a woman,

---

[10] De George, "Defining Moral Obligations," 23, 24–25. For responses from within the military, see *Army*, Feb. 1985, 5–6.

[11] Gerald Postema, "Moral Responsibility in Professional Ethics," *New York University Law Review* 55, 1 (Apr. 1980): 64.

[12] The large numbers of Iraqi soldiers killed by American and Allied forces in the recent conflict in the Persian Gulf caused widespread moral concern about

and the morals of the adult are not those of the child. . . . We find the differences of the sexes, of the ages, the difference that rises from a greater or lesser degree of kinship . . . all affect moral relations." Similarly, "as professors, we have duties which are not those of merchants. Those of the industrialist are quite different from those of the soldier, those of the soldier from those of the priest, and so on." But some duties are common to everyone; therefore, conflicts are inevitable: "the priest or soldier . . . have a wholly different duty [of] passive obedience . . . [and] it is the doctor's duty on occasion to lie." The upshot is that there are many kinds of morality, that "morality" needs specification: "We find within every society a plurality of morals that operate on parallel lines."[13] Professional codes fit neatly into such balkanized morality.

Durkheim's sweeping case for moral pluralism yields a curious vision of society. Its moral subsystems form "centres of moral life . . . which although bound up together, are distinct . . . [and yield] a kind of moral polymorphism." Without these different forms, he argues, we would have a "moral vacuum where the life-blood drains away even from individual morality," a system in which "the manufacturer, the workman, the employee, in carrying out his occupation, is aware of no influence set above him to check his egotism."[14] In other words, without the multiplicity of moral codes and social sanctions, people will act with unbridled selfishness. And against that threat, such codes are both morally protective and socially enriching.

Virginia Held approves the role moralities for a different reason:

For everyone to try to be equally concerned about the whole of morality all the time may lead to the dismissal of morality as hopelessly complicated, irrelevant, or vague. . . . A division of moral labor, both at the level of practice and at the level of theories about what the practice ought to be will have a better chance of leading to the improvement . . . [of] morality.

---

the disproportion of casualties. This shows dramatically the problems of the obligation of partiality in the military.

[13] Emile Durkheim, *Professional Ethics and Civic Morals*, trans. Cornelia Brookfield (Glencoe, Ill.: Free Press, 1958), 3–5.

[14] Ibid., 7, 12. Durkheim associates such moral codes with the guild system and the formation of *collegia* for workers, which functioned in Roman times and reappeared in the eleventh century to monitor the practices of people in various roles and take disciplinary measures against offenders; see, in particular, 17–22.

Further, she argues, "we are all occupants of a role," and once having decided on a role, "a person can often achieve more in that role . . . by concentrating on the manageable segment or moral concern reflected in the role than by trying to do the entire job of morality all at once." [15] Held treats morality as if it were a large and complex body of knowledge, like the whole of science, too large for one intelligence to comprehend [16]—another version of the simplicity argument.

However, Held offers a dramatic qualification to her endorsement of role morality: "The lawyer," she argues,

> ought to consider to what extent he or she has an obligation to further the major concern of the legal system to assure respect for moral rights. . . . At least some substantial part of the time, the lawyer ought to contribute to the objectives of the legal system as a whole, and the role of lawyer ought to call on lawyers to do so.

The lawyer has a larger responsibility than is dictated by service to clients, and it can even supersede the latter. "We can recognize that some potential clients are more worthy of winning in [the] . . . courts than others," and "the profession of lawyer should contribute to justice, as that of the physician to health." [17] A good lawyer takes care of her clients, but she is also responsible to the community for furthering justice. Unfortunately, Held doesn't say how she should balance these responsibilities. Further, in proposing that lawyers' actions be judged by a wider morality, Held raises doubts about the consistency of her view.

---

[15] Virginia Held, "The Division of Moral Labor and the Role of the Lawyer," in Luban, ed., *The Good Lawyer*, 64.

[16] Held goes further and says that "nearly all morality is role morality," depending on some distinctive background for the operation of its rules. She believes that "there is more danger in failing to see the roles that pervade so-called 'ordinary' morality than in failing to see the persons occupying the roles of doctor, lawyer, etc., as also persons"; ibid., 66–67. Her defense of the lawyer's role is oddly libertarian: "If those purchasing the service [of a lawyer] have a right to pursue their economic interests, they have a right to purchase legal services along with other goods, if lawyers have rights to supply these goods"; 68. It echoes the familiar economic plea for unfettered pursuit of self-interest. In another essay, however, she argues that differences in the way we justify conduct by appealing to different roles "is morally salutary" and provides "an institutional balance, or system of checks within the social system which each system [legal and political] exerts upon the other, allowing both . . . more nearly to approach moral justification than could either system alone"; "Justification: Legal and Political," *Ethics* 86 (1975): 11.

[17] Held, "Division," 68, 72, 77.

If distinct professional roles contribute to morality, they should not need criticism from a larger moral perspective, one she herself has argued is too unmanageable for a person to master.

In contrast to Held and Durkheim, John Simmons argues that many obligations of professions and jobs, "positional duties" he calls them, are not conceived as having moral force. While they are "requirements which must be met in order to fill some position successfully, not *all* such requirements are duties" of a moral kind. In general, positional duties lack moral force: "nonperformance of a positional duty may or may not make one vulnerable to coercive sanctions," but it would normally result in no more than "strong disapproval." The nonperformance is a "morally *neutral* fact."[18] Where someone is sent to carry out an order, Simmons states, there is usually no moral import. A delivery person sent out regularly with customers' orders, who one day refuses, has done nothing wrong morally. And a secretary whose job is to distribute mail, who one day throws it away, may be reprimanded or fired, but is not subject to moral censure. Or a lawyer neglecting to negotiate a deal for someone who is counting on it does nothing morally wrong. These are only failures of positional duties, not moral failures.

Simmons makes one important exception: the elected government representative who fails to carry out his work responsibilities *is* morally negligent. The difference stems from his having run for office. A negligent President "is blameworthy because he voluntarily entered his position and undertook, in full knowledge of the details of the situation, to perform the duties of that position. . . . He violated an obligation (of great importance) to perform his positional duties."[19]

I find Simmons's distinction unpersuasive. The secretary and the delivery boy also accept their jobs "voluntarily," and like the president "undertook, in full knowledge of the details of the situation, to perform the duties" of their positions. The lawyer does something similar when he accepts his commission, the military officer when he accepts his. So how distinguish between the failure of the President and that of other persons along the lines of accepted responsibilities? The President's case

---

[18]John Simmons, *Moral Principles and Political Obligations* (Princeton, N.J.: Princeton University Press, 1979), 17, 21.
[19]Ibid., 19.

turns on the point that artificial persons are morally culpable if, *understanding what is required*, they fail to carry out the duties of their jobs. But does this not put moral significance into nearly all jobs? A military example shows the point nicely: a soldier's failure to carry out orders may be tantamount to rebellion or insurrection. Other members of his force depend on him and he bears a heavy responsibility to them.[20] It is foolish to call this obligation morally neutral. Other jobs too involve trust and dependence in some degree, regarding not only an employer but other workers and even the consumers who use one's product.[21] At what point does such dependence become nonmoral?

IV

Consider one systematic way of putting responsibility into a tight framework of roles. The Japanese have a practice of placing responsibility at the top with the person in charge—for example, the officer overseeing and directing operations in a corporation. The president of an unprofitable company resigns "or the board of directors of a bank in which fraud has occurred dock their own salaries to pay for the default." Rodney Clark calls this "symbolic responsibility" and explains that "the rules of this kind of responsibility are simple, for it comes automatically with high position. When something goes wrong the senior man or group of men presiding over the mistake will 'take responsibility' to lift the blame from their subordinates."[22] The process works in Japanese politics, or did, much the same way

[20] The obligation of military personnel to obey is qualified by the condition that orders must be legal—among other things, in accord with the rules of war as defined by international agreements. See Chapter 4, section III for a discussion of individual responsibility in the military context.

[21] One thinks here of the importance of "whistle blowers" in work contexts and of their duty *not* to do what they are told, what they agreed to in their original contracts. The engineers who warned Morton Thiokol before the tragic Challenger launch and Karen Silkwood in the Oklahoma nuclear facility are good examples. These duties don't vitiate the moral force of work duties, but supplement them.

[22] Rodney Clark, *The Japanese Company* (New Haven, Conn.: Yale University Press, 1979), 125. Dennis Thompson, writing about the American political context, might call this "the ritual taking of responsibility." He argues that the *point* of it often has nothing to do with taking responsibility in the usual sense; *Political Ethics and Public Office* (Cambridge, Mass.: Harvard University Press, 1987), 43–45.

as in business.[23] Blaming the leader, like piling sins on a ritual goat, relieves others of guilt. "When a mistake is made the resignation, transfer or other penance of the leader of the group allows everyone to make a fresh start"; it helps the organization keep functioning.[24] But suppose the leader had no idea that mistakes were being made? In that case "symbolic responsibility need not . . . have much to do with what one could call 'real responsibility', the moral and practical accountability for decisions and events. . . . The manager who is transferred because production was lost when someone misread the instructions on a machine and stripped its cogs will soon be given a new and important assignment."[25] In the meantime, the real culprit will find himself under a cloud even though he isn't charged formally.

At one level of this arrangement, responsibility is placed and punishment meted out whether it is personally deserved or not. The premise is that *someone* must take responsibility for a mistake, and the practice is to blame the person on top. But if that person is not at fault, adjustments will be made, the practice notwithstanding.

The confusion generated by symbolic responsibility can be discerned in American corporations, where, as one corporate manager complains, "you are judged on *results* whether those results are your fault or not." This lack of control evokes in response a strategy to diffuse responsibility and so avoid victimization. "People . . . avoid putting things clearly in writing. They try to make group decisions so that responsibility is not always clearly defined." Thus, "If I tell you what to do, I can't bawl you out if things don't work. And this is why a lot of bosses don't give explicit directions. They just give a statement of objectives, and then they can criticize subordinates who fail to make their goals." The author who records this observes that in a corporate structure "pushing down details relieves superiors of the

[23] It may be that more recently the morality of Japanese politicians is treated more in the Western fashion, which, as I argue, by the nature of its coming out of the tradition of agency, is entirely problematic.

[24] Those in charge are also sometimes penalized financially. An instance is Mazda's move to cut executives' salaries temporarily in response to proof of company neglect regarding a mechanical problem in the company's cars; *San Francisco Chronicle*, Dec. 27, 1990, C 4.

[25] Clark, *The Japanese Company*, 126.

burden of too much knowledge, particularly guilty knowledge." In these arrangements, "credit flows up" while "responsibility for decisions and profits is pushed as far down the organizational line as possible." This encourages the "fragmentation of consciousness" often characteristic of corporations.[26] Thus, in effect, making people accountable for what they don't do may work toward a loss of responsibility altogether.

The need to hold someone responsible when corporate deeds are criticized may lead to a curious perversion of attitudes toward moral responsibility, as one comment by a corporate official illustrates. "I've often thought," he says, "that we should appoint a position entitled Chief Fall Guy. Joking, of course. But it would be a good idea. He would be well-paid; plenty of benefits. And if things go wrong, he would go to jail or whatever, and his family would be provided for."[27]

Although the military also illustrates a hierarchical structure where responsibility goes "automatically with high position," here even the distinction between symbolic and real responsibility may be hard to draw. For instance, during the American war trials in Japan at least two Japanese officers were found guilty because they held "command responsibility" for atrocities in Bataan; yet it was acknowledged that they could not control their troops. Thus, if culpability derived from their place in the pyramid, why shouldn't the emperor have been convicted as well, or even in their place? Sir William Webb, the Australian head of the tribunal, reasoned that Hirohito's "authority was required for the war. If he did not want war he should have withheld his authority." To which William Manchester adds: "It is difficult to understand why if Hirohito was to be spared, his generals should have to die."[28] Are we to infer that only Hirohito and none of the others was really culpable, then? That seems too simple. On the other hand, if we cannot trace responsibility to the commander-in-chief, then how can we trace it in a democracy to the citizens who stand behind their commander? Re-

[26]Robert Jackall, *Moral Mazes* (New York: Oxford University Press, 1988), 70, 79, 20, 21, 17, 84.
[27]Ibid., 85.
[28]Sir William Webb in *An Introduction to Japan* (1957), cited in William Manchester, *American Caesar: Douglas MacArthur 1880–1964* (Boston: Little, Brown, 1978), 485, 486. Also see Philip Picagallo, *The Japanese on Trial* (Austin: University of Texas Press, 1979), 123–24.

sponsibility has gotten lost despite the unambiguous line of authority.

That problems of responsibility are endemic in the military became clear through the Nuremberg trials, after which American military law was revised to make individual soldiers legally responsible for their actions *even when they acted under orders.*[29] They became responsible for the conformity of their actions, and their orders, to the international codes of war their country agreed to. The consequences for an error of judgment about this may be severe, and responsibility is at the individual's door. But both by training and by oath soldiers are obligated to obey. They are thus put in a doubly vulnerable position. "Does that requirement place individual soldiers in situations that they may perceive as moral dilemmas?" Col. Anthony Hartle asks, and answers, "It may, but the policy of insisting on individual responsibility remains morally necessary."[30] It is morally necessary because, under the practice of legally prosecuting foreign military personnel for offenses, responsibility *must* be given a location; consistency requires it.

The tension between the demand for responsibility on one side and the nature of military training on the other is particularly troubling, to Wasserstrom among others. He observes that "it may conceptually make no sense to think of an army in which each individual endeavors to reason about and resolve questions of how morally to behave. . . . One would no longer have an army and would, instead, have only a very different kind of col-

[29] Telford Taylor writes that during World War I both American and British army manuals put responsibility on those giving illegal orders but not on subordinates carrying them out. Actions on orders from either "government" or "commanders" were exempted from responsibility. Taylor says these provisions "raised questions whether anyone at all could be held liable if the 'commanders' were themselves acting under orders from still farther up the military chain of command"; *Nuremberg and Vietnam: An American Tragedy* (Chicago: Quadrangle Books, 1970), 184–85. Anthony Hartle seems to deny this, saying that the "American PME [professional military ethic] traditionally has not accepted or condoned stereotypical obedience to orders" even though it may appear otherwise; *Moral Issues*, 127. While the burden of proof does rest with the one who refuses to obey, the code suggests that "the fact that the individual was acting pursuant to orders may be considered in mitigation of punishment," which is to say it counts as extenuation; see U.S. Army Regulations, FM 27-10. Hartle gives an account of the provisions of the Laws of War and discusses problems connected with them; see particularly *Moral Issues*, 70–84.

[30] Ibid., 128. Hartle doesn't explain whether the dilemmas are only apparent or might be real.

lection of persons."[31] Hartle seems to agree, but wisely does not expect a professional ethic to simplify this picture: "Succinct, absolute norms simplify the moral universe. . . . But in the case of the military professional, simplification would create an unacceptable threat to the very values that the American military exists to protect."[32] That is to say, the military needs to share the community values it is committed to protect, even though this means burdening soldiers in extraordinary ways.

In dealing with the dual requirements—military discipline on one side and responsibility for his actions on the other—a soldier might seem to need, as de George suggests, a remarkably clear moral perception and a steady character. Adm. James Stockdale would agree, having once told West Point cadets, "I say it's your duty to be a moralist."[33] But, however sound, such advice does not assist in managing the complicated military universe and its moral dilemmas.

v

Moral ambiguity in the military context stems in part from the fact those receiving the orders are in the circumstances of action while those issuing them stay at a distance. For example, the military order, "Take the bridge" leaves the means entirely open. "Take it without loss of civilian life" tightens the conditions, but still leaves the means open. Unlike the purposeful ambiguity of the corporate manager's orders, the ambiguity of military orders is often inherent. The one giving the order lacks detailed knowledge of the scene; he may have no exact intention about how the order should be executed—only a vague idea, roughly conceived. The details need to be filled in by those at the scene. But predictably this creates problems, and nowhere more clearly than in the military.

Consider the Malmédy incident in World War II, which con-

[31] Wasserstrom, "Roles and Morality," 31.

[32] Hartle, *Moral Issues*, 119. There seems to be tension between Hartle's idea of the trust given to the military, i.e., to protect public values by force, and de George's idea that the public trust requires the military to cultivate peaceableness.

[33] See James Stockdale, *A Vietnam Experience* (Stanford, Calif.: Hoover Press, 1984), 72. Stockdale stresses the need for a firm moral character in the event one is taken prisoner of war.

cerned a German unit that was pressed to move quickly and therefore massacred its prisoners of war. The bodies were found later in the snow, many frozen with their hands up. It was graphic and unequivocal proof of violation of the Geneva Convention.[34] How did it happen? A German soldier testified that an order came from a meeting of German commanders that "we should behave toward the enemy in such a way that we create amongst them panic and terror and that the reputation for spreading panic and terror . . . should precede our troops, so that the enemy should be frightened even to meet them."[35] Creating panic and terror is a broad description of purpose which needs translation into specifics. In the present case the officer of the German unit repeated this order to his company along with additional instruction to behave brutally with the enemy, and he added the threat of harsh discipline for any who disobeyed.[36]

Was the order to terrify impermissible, given the context of war? American officers themselves denied that it was: "To create fright and terror in the minds of the enemy and thus break his will to resist must be the aim of any attacking army." American officers acknowledged that the right of prisoners to proper care is "not absolute"; according to Lt. Col. John Dwinell, a counsel for the defense, "there is a notable exception to [the] rule, 'when

[34] How did political and military leaders generally view the force of the Geneva Convention in critical situations during World War II? British authorities instructed their commandos to "never give the enemy a chance; the days when we could practice the rules of sportsmanship are over. For the time being every soldier must be a potential gangster and must be prepared to adopt their methods"; quoted in Plinio Prioreschi, *Man and War* (New York: Philosophical Library, 1986), 180. As to the strictures of international law, one remembers that Churchill advocated mining Norwegian waters, arguing that "our defeat would mean an age of barbaric violence. . . . [Thus] acting in the name of the Covenant, we have a right, indeed we are bound in duty, to abrogate for a space some of the conventions of the very laws we seek to . . . reaffirm." Chancellor von Bethmann Hollweg of World War I is more open when he admits that German troops have invaded Belgium: "Gentlemen, that is a breach of international law. . . . We were forced to ignore the rightful protests of the Government of Belgium. The wrong—I speak openly—the wrong we thereby commit we will try to make good as soon as our military aims have been attained." Both these examples quoted by Prioreschi, 167, 182.

[35] James Weingartner, *Crossroads of Death* (Berkeley: University of California Press, 1979), 77.

[36] It is related that the officer informed his men that those who showed consideration for the enemy would be shown no consideration by him and that he expressed his displeasure toward one subordinate by requiring him to "go into battle exposed on the hull of a tank"; ibid., 81–82.

the achievement of victory would be hindered . . . by stopping to give quarter.' " It was also acknowledged that the mission of the German group was jeopardized by caring for the prisoners. What was wrong then?

The Allied court hearing the case declared that the German officer "was criminally liable in that he had omitted giving his subordinates specific orders concerning the disposition of prisoners of war. It had, therefore, been left to the discretion of soldiers of lesser rank whether to permit themselves to be burdened by prisoners, thus, possibly, jeopardizing their missions."[37] The court's decision to hold the officer responsible is understandable, given the context and the details. It charged him with failure to "give specific orders" instead of passing along the ones he received, but that hardly seems like a crime.[38] Figuring out how to interpret instructions presents a difficulty to anyone, and distance from the source of the instruction enhances it. The question is how those at the scene should understand orders given by someone unfamiliar with their circumstances. And conversely, how are those giving orders to foresee the choices and obstacles that will face their agents? The answer to both questions is that they cannot understand, not fully, and that means that the gap cannot be closed.

VI

When a wrong or injustice is done, we want to know where responsibility lies. We search for *someone* accountable, refuse to accept an agentless wrong. Yet the arrangement of artificial persons encourages moral frustration and agentless deeds. The problem is clear in bureaucracies. Hannah Arendt, who calls bureaucracy "the most formidable form" of government, explains that

bureaucracy [is] the rule of an intricate system of bureaus in which no men, neither one nor the best, neither the few nor the many, can be held responsible, and which could be properly called rule by No-

---

[37] Ibid., 181, 156, 61, 181–82.

[38] De George proposes that "military professionals *are* responsible not only for their own actions but for the chain of actions they initiate. . . . Commanders must, from a moral point of view, care how a job gets done"; "Defining Moral Obligations," 29. This means, I infer, that he would include such a requirement in an ethical code; yet, as I argue, this solution is simplistic.

body. . . . Rule by Nobody is clearly the most tyrannical of all, since there is no one left who could even be asked to answer for what is being done.[39]

The multiplicity of agents and of their roles protects people in bureaucracies and insures that Nobody does whatever is done. The arrangement leads a chase through warrens and thickets of roles, instructions, interpretations and chains of command. With increasing distance between order and action, with the attendant increase in ambiguity, responsibility is harder to retrieve from the cracks. Thus, it seems that institutions themselves are the problem, and that, as David Luban says, "moral responsibility is itself diminished or 'divided down' by institutional structure."[40]

Consider this loss of responsibility in the light of a story in Plato's *Republic*. The story tells how Gyges, a shepherd, came accidentally upon a ring that could make him invisible. With the ring protecting him from discovery, he entered the palace, seduced the Queen in her chambers, conspired with her to kill the king, and then he assumed the throne. Glaucon tells the story to show how *everyone* would act if they could get away with it. He argues that, given such an opportunity, no one would "refrain his hands from the possessions of others and not touch them, though he might with impunity take what he wished from the market place, and enter into houses and lie with whom he pleased, and slay and loose from bonds whomsoever he would, and in all other things conduct himself among mankind as the equal of a god."[41] Gyges' invisibility cuts his actions loose from accountability, gives him a chance to do what he pleases with impunity. It satisfies a common fantasy of being able to act without regard for rules of decency or the effects of one's actions on others, a vision of egotism, power, and free-wheeling self-indulgence.

[39] Hannah Arendt, *On Violence* (New York: Harcourt, Brace & World, 1970), 38–39.

[40] David Luban, "The Adversary System Excuse," in Luban, ed., *The Good Lawyer*, 103. A parallel discussion of responsibility in government and the military is presented in Luban, "The Legacies of Nuremberg," *Social Research* 54: 4 (Winter 1987).

[41] Plato, *The Republic*, trans. Paul Shorey, in *The Collected Dialogues of Plato*, ed. E. Hamilton and H. Cairns (Princeton, N.J.: Princeton University Press, 1961), 360b–c.

Glaucon challenges Socrates to refute this account of human nature. But I suggest this story also illustrates the situation of artificial persons. For roles and the complexity of institutional contexts bring a kind of moral invisibility to their possessors, and this in turn makes actions agentless, the deeds of Nobody.

VII

People who take responsibility in a context where it is avoidable, perhaps hazarding personal loss, win our applause. Consider as an example Dietrich von Choltitz, the German general Hitler placed in charge of occupied Paris. Hitler was faced with growing pessimism, disloyalty, and lack of discipline in the ranks; von Choltitz was a dedicated officer who "never questioned an order no matter how harsh it was." He had shown his mettle by the punitive measures he took against Rotterdam and in his scorched earth retreat at Sebastopol. Von Choltitz was a natural choice, an officer of "irreproachable loyalty" who "would restore discipline to the city with an iron hand."[42]

Repeatedly during von Choltitz's brief command of nineteen days, Hitler sent him orders that he was to remain "master of the situation," to hold the city "at any price"; and if defense became hopeless, to destroy it, raze it, turn it to a pile of ruins. Hitler's policy for Paris was "limited scorched earth"; if he couldn't keep Paris, he would deprive the rest of the world of its artistic and historical treasures.[43] For von Choltitz two things cast a shadow of doubt over these instructions and over the policy he had first thought to be "perfectly sound." One was Hitler's hysterical behavior during the initial briefing, which made von Choltitz question his leader's rationality. Hitler's plan for Paris was, he concluded, to "devastate the city 'and then sit in its ashes and accept the consequences,'" a policy von Choltitz thought vengeful and pointless. The other factor was the passionate plea of the mayor of Paris. "Often," the mayor argued, "it is given to a general to destroy, rarely to preserve. Imagine that in the future . . . you might be able to say, 'One day I could have destroyed all this, and I preserved it as a gift for humanity.'

[42] Larry Collins and Dominique Lapierre, *Is Paris Burning?* (New York: Simon & Schuster, 1965), 31, 32.
[43] Ibid., 123, 167, 176.

General, is not that worth all a conqueror's glory? "[44] In the end, von Choltitz saw himself as controlling a world treasure and being ordered to do what history would condemn him for.

Von Choltitz's upbringing, his training, his personality, all inclined him to obey orders: "He had always been firmly locked inside Germany's impersonal military machine. His [major] decisions . . . had always been made for him." Personally he did not like making major decisions but preferred to postpone them. For him this was "an appalling dilemma":

That history would never forgive the man who destroyed Paris was a persuasive argument to von Choltitz; that the man who did it might be hanged in its ashes was more convincing. Von Choltitz was prepared to die as a soldier in Paris, but not as a criminal. That night . . . he . . . remarked, "And I will sit on the last bridge and blow myself up along with it, because it will be the only thing left for me."[45]

Von Choltitz faced a complex net of conflicts between duties. One duty was defined by his long-standing commitment as an officer to his military leader. Another was more difficult to define. He thought of it as a duty to the world, to history. But what kind of duty is owed to the world, or to history, or one's self-respect? What role would explain or require it? The obligation is real, but the term "role" is unhelpful in understanding it. A third factor, the obligations of husband and father, enhanced his dilemma. For under the Nazi *Sippenhaft* law his family could be punished for his failures as a general; they were "the hostages of the state, the guarantors of a general's good conduct." If a general failed and was taken prisoner, his family might even be executed.[46] It was a law enacted to persuade someone wavering, someone in precisely von Choltitz's position.

Von Choltitz stalled the destruction of Paris by various means and at the end pleaded with the Allied forces to invade the city promptly to save it. There ensued a brief battle with modest damage, and as he prepared to surrender von Choltitz felt

he had nothing . . . for which to reproach himself. His soldiers were at this moment executing the orders of the Fuehrer to "fight to their last

[44] Ibid., 68, 90, 128–29, 176.

[45] Ibid., 41.

[46] Von Choltitz, who had three children, was angered at the *Sippenhaft* law and commented that "if Germany was using practices like that, she was returning to the Middle Ages"; ibid. I discuss such practices and their connection with responsibility in Chapter 8.

cartridges." His soldier's honor was intact. . . . At the same time, he could now await the judgment of history without fear or shame. . . . In these last moments of liberty, von Choltitz felt with perfect sincerity that he had properly served his name and his nation in Paris.

This sanguine view of his honor was not shared by other German officers, one of whom requested the Reich Tribunal to open criminal proceedings against him for having "failed to live up to what was expected of him" as the general defending Paris.[47] For he did fail, and deliberately, to do his duty as an officer. The question for him was not whether that was a duty, but whether there was a compelling reason not to do it.

Von Choltitz's case shows that something is wrong with the concept of roles as a framework for discussing moral responsibility. It is tempting to define the problem he faced as a conflict among the duties of citizen and father, of trusted military officer, and of what might be called his role in the world and history. But what, precisely, *is* his duty as a citizen? Or as a father, since his own honor is tied to his family's? And one's "role" in history cannot be defined as a *role* at all, no more than it is a role to be in a demographic category. Why then should this nebulous, questionable "role" in history take precedence over the others whose lines were clearer? In terms of roles, von Choltitz's decision looks foolhardy. The reality was that von Choltitz had to consider his responsibility to people on many sides, some close to him, others who gave him official trust, still others unknown and unconnected with him. To come to this judgment he had to put aside "role duties" and deal with his position as an agent negotiating a number of claims on him. Seeing the conflict as a conflict of roles invites the question, which role has precedence, which is most important? But this question depersonalizes the decision, as if it were not uniquely von Choltitz's to make, as if it were only a matter of following set rules. It is partly the fact that it *was his* decision, and that it fell outside the rules, that brings him honor.

One finds similar examples in the corporate arena. Robert Jackall tells the story of a man whom he calls "Brady," an English chartered accountant, which is "a profession that [Brady] values highly and one that carries considerably more status, respect,

[47] Ibid., 296, 343.

and public trust in Britain than its American equivalent." When Brady became a company vice president in America, he found irregularities in the company's practices and made full report of them to the president. Eventually there were criminal charges brought against the company, upon which Brady's peers accused him of disloyalty to the company. His reaction was: "I was in jeopardy of violating my professional code. And I feel that you have to stick up for that. If your profession has standing, it has that standing because *someone stood up for it.*" Brady's role as vice president and his former role as a chartered accountant do not explain his actions or his determination to adhere to a moral standard.[48]

Strange things happen to moral responsibility in highly structured organizations. It tends to become diffused and, if it is insisted on, corrupted. Many problems result from the definition of roles and their specific requirements, as well as from the crucial ambiguity of orders. We will meet all these issues again. Chapter 3 looks more closely at roles and at how they skew our perspective. Chapter 4 then tries to get to some moral roots of the problem.

[48] Jackall, *Moral Mazes*, 105, 109. In the light of the difficulty of taking personal responsibility in the military, even Hermann Goering's claim at the Nuremberg trials about the Anschluss is commendable: "I take one hundred per cent responsibility. . . . I ignored the Fuehrer's opposition and led everything to its final stage of development"; quoted in Masao Maruyama, *Thought and Behavior in Modern Japanese Politics* (London: Oxford University Press, 1963), 100.

THREE

Roles

Am I not Christopher Sly, old Sly's son of Burton Heath; by birth a ped-
lar, by education a cardmaker, by transmutation a bearherd, and now by
present profession a tinker?   Shakespeare, *Taming of the Shrew*

REPRESENTING OTHERS, onstage or in professions, means
having a role: that is Hobbes's idea. But if representing imposes
a role, so do countless other functions and positions: sales-
person, business executive, public official, teacher. Each has its
internal requirements, its rules and imperatives that lack force
in other contexts. There is therefore a special tension between a
person and her role, and the question arises how the role relates
to the person in it. We ask whether there is a natural person who
occupies her various roles, and if so, what scope for action that
natural person has.

I

The paradigmatic role is, as Hobbes says, theatrical. An actor
represents someone real or fictional; he speaks lines, expresses
feelings, adopts mannerisms; he moves and gestures as the
stage directions dictate, all in an effort to represent his character
in the dramatic situation. Onstage the actor *is* the person he
plays, but that identification is, of course, fictional; the play is a
created and fictional world, in which the actor is not responsible
for what his character does or says. If he strikes or kills or deceives, signs orders, makes promises he doesn't keep—all while
playing his part—these misdeeds are not his. But if his stage
actions are not his, they aren't anyone's. One can go further:
they are only in a tenuous sense *actions* since they occur onstage.

How can they compare with actions in work or professional roles?

An actor has to do things he would never do offstage, things foreign to his taste and character; he is required not to be himself. Then is he involved in these actions? The answer must be yes. Yet once he is in the part, a paradoxical relation connects his integrity as actor to his integrity as person, for his very willingness to do onstage things that he would shrink from offstage belongs to his integrity as an actor. Dissembling is his profession; does he then have integrity or not? If his performance isn't mechanical, then even as he acts and pretends, he *is* an actor profoundly engrossed in that role. That is who he is.

There is a difference between an actor and, say, a confidence artist who deceives others for gain. For while an actor's dissembling is redeemed by his profession, the confidence man's dishonesty is not; nor is a thief's dishonesty redeemed by his. Thus, the dissembling of an actor—some would say of other professionals as well—stands in a distinctive relation to his character. It lacks power to hurt his moral stature and may even enhance it. We will return to this later.

Describing the actor's situation is difficult partly because actions on the stage are a special kind, or are actions in a special sense. Onstage the actor cannot sign papers legally, though he can sign them in his part; his character signs them, one might say. On the other hand, he isn't detached from his role either; he must become the person he plays. His ability to be absorbed in the role is part of his skill, and how thoroughly he takes on the part and absorbs himself in it, reflects on his quality as an actor. Thus, being an actor in a part seems to mean having two identities, one onstage and another off. This seems clearest when, as he leaves the theater, he must switch from acting or being X to acting or being himself. He removes one hat and puts on another.

On this way of describing the situation, however, an actor really has two roles, the one he plays onstage and that of himself. *Whatever* he does he does in one role or the other, he is never out of roles, offstage or on, at work, at leisure, at home. Extending this picture, we are all, at every moment, captive to some role. A waiter goes home to a different persona; the business executive takes on the role of understanding father; the lawyer turns with another face to improving his community.

11

A person chooses an occupational role and performs in it better or worse, adapts to it more or less, and can leave it. But while in the role she changes her behavior and her ways of relating to others, and like the actor, she does things she would not do otherwise. That change is morally troubling, Sartre argues in his discussion of "bad faith":

> Let us consider this waiter in the café. His movement is quick and forward, a little too precise, a little too rapid. He comes toward the patrons with a step a little too quick. He leans forward a little too eagerly; his voice, his eyes express an interest a little too solicitous for the order of the customers. . . . All his behavior seems to us a game. He applies himself to chaining his movements as if they were mechanisms. . . . He is playing at *being* a waiter in a café. . . . This obligation is not different from that which is imposed on all tradesmen. Their condition is wholly one of ceremony. . . . There is the dance of the grocer, of the tailor, of the auctioneer, by which they endeavor to persuade their clientele that they are nothing but a grocer, an auctioneer, a tailor. . . . Society demands that [the grocer] limit himself to his function as a grocer, just as the soldier at attention makes himself into a soldier-thing with a direct regard which does not see at all. . . . There are many precautions to imprison a man in what he is, as if we lived in perpetual fear that he might escape from it, that he might break away and suddenly elude his condition.[1]

People in various kinds of work, even entrepreneurs, put on a performance for others. The waiter acts different, thinking of himself as a waiter, and by his manner deceives others about himself and his feelings. He may be an excellent waiter, but because of that he is a prisoner of his role, and being a prisoner he shows bad faith, Sartre argues. He thinks of himself as he is not, like a coward who exhibits bad faith in denying to himself that he is a coward.

Sartre thinks that a person's moral freedom depends on recognizing herself as she is and her choices for what they are; he believes there is an obligation to be sincere and not to fool others or ourselves, an obligation to honesty that is connected to recognizing that being free to make choices entails responsibility for having chosen. Roles, in asking us to pretend, undermine a sense of responsibility. Thus, waiters, grocers, and others who

[1] Jean-Paul Sartre, *Being and Nothingness*, trans. Hazel Barnes (New York: Washington Square Press, 1966), 101–2.

take their roles seriously are not much different from actors, pretending to feel what they don't feel, making choices they wouldn't otherwise. But, on the other hand, their bad faith isn't optional as things stand, for they need to practice appropriate forms of dissembling to do their jobs well, and people count on them to do it.[2]

Sartre believes a person ought to be authentic, but how is this to be understood? He writes:

> The waiter in the café can not be immediately a café waiter in the sense that this inkwell *is* an inkwell, or the glass is a glass. . . . He knows well what it "means". . . . He knows the rights which it allows. . . . But all these concepts . . . refer to the transcendent. It is a matter . . . of rights and duties conferred on a "person possessing rights." And it is precisely this person *who I have to be* (if I am the waiter in question) and who I am not. It is not that I do not wish to be this person or that I want this person to be different. But rather there is no common measure between his being and mine. It is a "representation" for others and for myself, which means that I can be he only in *representation*. But if I represent myself as him, I am not he. . . . I can not be he, I can only play *at being* him. . . . In vain do I fulfill the functions of the café waiter. I can be he only in the neutralized mode, as the actor is Hamlet. . . . Yet there is no doubt that I *am* in a sense a café waiter—otherwise could I not just as well call myself a diplomat or a reporter? . . . I am a waiter in the mode of *being what I am not*.[3]

The waiter in the café is not a waiter *essentially*, yet being an actor playing a part is the only way to be a waiter: one cannot be really a waiter or really himself.[4] Now, Sartre argues, rights and other moral terms apply uniquely to *persons*. Thus it follows that, insofar as being a waiter requires behaving as one is not, it means avoiding the rights and responsibilities of a person. Like the actor, the waiter's integrity depends on his disingenuousness and pretense, which means that his integrity is forfeit.

Performing a job well, making an effort to do what a good waiter or actor does, usually reflects credit on one. But Sartre's

[2] See Peter Caws's account of this in his *Sartre* (London: Routledge & Kegan Paul, 1979), esp. 76–77.

[3] Sartre, *Being and Nothingness*, 102–3.

[4] One might invoke the philosophical distinction between the 'is' of predication and the 'is' of identity here, for the man who waits tables *is* a waiter in the predicate sense, though not *identified* with the waiter job. But, as my subsequent argument shows, this is insufficient to explain the problems caused by such roles for identity.

point is that doing so means a person's choices and actions are not his, and thus he doesn't feel responsible for them. Through the role he forfeits taking responsibility for himself.

III

The terminology of roles thus brings with it an unsettling ambiguity about identity. The waiter *is* a waiter; he is a person who works at that job. But while the first phrase might suggest identity of self and role, the second implies a separation between them. If the waiter leaves this job and takes another—if he becomes a salesman, say—then he will *be* a salesman in exactly the sense in which he is now a waiter. Is this a change in identity? If not, must he have an identity independent of his jobs or roles? And how is that referred to? The good actor is adaptable to a role, can identify with different characters; but to adapt oneself and have a role means to be separate from it, to be a person who can *have* it.[5] And both waiter and actor would distinguish who they are from their roles, even though they identify with their roles *while in them*. Perhaps, then, each has a double identity.

On one level such a division of persona seems innocuous. Most work and professional roles require some dissembling: teachers and doctors need to appear patient, responsive, and authoritative. Even the non-work roles of friend, parent, spouse, committee member have their demands, and in all these roles we try to live up to what is expected of us. We daily dissemble and deceive, we do what being a such-and-such requires, and we excuse our insincerity by appealing to the roles themselves.

The waiter has a bad day, is in a bad mood, yet he seems cheerful. The business man bluffs through a problematic situation. Sartre asks: "Under these conditions what can be the sig-

[5] Phyllis Morris connects a change of identity with roles in her *Sartre's Concept of a Person: An Analytic Approach* (Amherst: University of Massachusetts Press, 1976) 80–81, 92–93. She writes that a "person may in one sense truly say of himself 'I am a thief' when the pattern is firmly established, but if he should reform and become an honest man, the 'I' which is the body-subject persists. 'I' cannot, then, refer unequivocally to the body-subject"; 92. Morris contrasts body-subject to character in Sartre's analysis: "In one sense the person is the body *qua* conscious subject. In another sense, a person is the pattern or system of conscious relations that this body has with other objects and with others through time"; 81.

nificance of the ideal of sincerity except as a task impossible to achieve of which the very meaning is in contradiction with the structure of my consciousness. To be sincere . . . is to be what one is."[6] Then sincerity and conscientious work appear irreconcilable.

The effort to fill a role may require great discipline and self-criticism, even a reshaping of oneself. A business manager who wants to succeed "dispassionately takes stock of himself," one scholar relates; "he analyzes his strengths and weaknesses . . . and then he systematically undertakes a program to reconstruct his image."[7] Since the role-holder here decides his own strategies and sets his goals, the distinction between role and private self becomes fuzzy; the two merge uneasily into one another. As a result, sincerity becomes hard even to define.

Sincerity also may not always be the preeminent virtue Sartre claims it to be, as in the cases of John Alden and Sir Tristan, each sent on an errand of great trust and delicacy. In "bad faith" Alden pleaded Miles Standish's case and put aside his own feelings from loyalty and the responsibility of his trust, while Tristan with full sincerity put aside his vow and friendship with the king to plead his own cause.[8] Both men bore some responsibility for their actions, but Alden's "bad faith" is surely a virtue while Tristan's "sincerity" is betrayal.[9] This shows that Sartre's moral condemnation of bad faith needs rethinking.

IV

An Elizabethan text describes the obligations of a wife: she "must have a speciall care to be silent, and to speake as seldome as she may, unless it be to hir husband, or at his bidding. . . . She must bestow as much time as she can steale from domesticall affaires, in the studie of notable sayings, and of the morall sentences of auncient Sages and good men."[10] The author pre-

---

[6] Sartre, *Being and Nothingness*, 105–6.

[7] Robert Jackall, *Moral Mazes* (New York: Oxford University Press, 1988), 59.

[8] The issue changes if Isolde took the love potion by accident, as some versions of the story say.

[9] The romantic tradition's glorification of Tristan's overwhelming passion doesn't soften his betrayal of a sacred trust, it seems to me.

[10] From Pierre de la Primaudaye, *The French Academie*, quoted in Thomas van Laan, *Role Playing in Shakespeare* (Toronto: University of Toronto Press, 1978), 18.

scribes a program for her: be quiet and read as much uplifting literature as possible. Nonetheless she has latitude in interpreting her role, more than is usually given an actor.[11] Many choices are open, and more striking, her role is seamlessly joined to the rest of her life. It is not like a hat she puts on at eight and takes off at five; depending on what other positions she has, she may be always in it. Yet she may have other roles running concurrently—like being a mother and a daughter—which are again seamlessly joined together. But where there is such proliferation of roles, that merge into one another and merge with the identity of the person in them, the role terminology seems to break down. One no longer wants to separate person and role in the way that the concepts require.

Perhaps we could distinguish two kinds of roles, one of which, such as waiter or actor, doesn't enter into one's identity. Its requirements and constraints have little influence on other roles or other aspects of life. The other kind stems from relationships so fundamental that we are identified by them. Most work roles would fall in the first class, while family relations are clearly in the second.

Consider the sixteenth-century role of king of England. Being king stemmed from an accident of birth, but required many specific duties: there were things a king must do, clothes he must wear, formalities to observe, ways of behaving. He had a ceremonial role much like an actor. But filling the role of king meant more than observing formalities, more than speaking and acting with a kingly tone and demeanor.

Now consider Richard III in Shakespeare's portrait, the very model of a bad king. His behavior is objectionable, writes Thomas van Laan, "not only because it is evil but also because it

[11]I mean "role" to incorporate some recognizable obligations, expectations and requirements. Van Laan says of his use: "I do not have in mind . . . that of a part in a play whose every word, gesture, and movement have been established . . . nor . . . do I mean anything so vague and general as the . . . loose sense of the term, in which everything we do becomes a role"; ibid., 19. Thus it might be argued that in modern American society, there is no role of wife, or perhaps that there are many forms to such a role. However loose, this ordinary sense is preferable to such technical sociological ones as Bruce Biddle's: "Role theory . . . is a science concerned with the study of behaviors that are characteristic of persons within contexts and with various processes that presumably produce, explain, or are affected by those behaviors"; *Role Theory: Expectations, Identities, and Behaviors* (New York: Academic Press, 1979), 4.

violates his office. The stress on his misbehavior thus keeps in focus a role-like quality of this office . . . the accumulated repertory of moves proper to kingship and obligatory for every occupant of the office." Richard has a clear understanding of the formalities required of him. He falls short "by conflicting with, and often inverting, the moves proper to" his role, while he "publicly pretends to play . . . 'the wise king's part'." It is precisely the "discrepancy between the actor and his part" that is Richard's failing, van Laan says.[12] He masters the forms and appearances while he pursues deceit, and thus does *not* satisfy the role. For the role of king has a moral component, and really filling it means having integrity and honor, means *not* playing a part. So while in one sense Richard is a model king and behaves as being king requires, in the larger meaning he fails in the role: "It may be that he cannot properly fulfill the kingly office because he is already entirely taken up with the role of King," van Laan comments.[13]

It is clear that some roles cannot be neatly detached from the role-holder and his character, that some roles are essentially joined to a person, and that a person of the wrong kind will fail in such a role no matter how carefully he performs the specifics it requires. Susan Wolf argues for an important difference between professions on these lines: "An inquiry into whether someone is a good artist, chemist, or typist will typically reveal nothing about a person's moral character or his or her obedience to moral principles. The examination of traits necessary for determining whether a person is a good rabbi, teacher, or politician, on the other hand, is apt to reveal quite a lot."[14] With a

[12]Van Laan, *Role Playing in Shakespeare*, 119. Van Laan sees the middle histories of Shakespeare as all focusing on the office of king both as a role and as requiring a person of character; 118.

[13]Ibid., 120. Van Laan calls attention to the way Margaret, whose daughter Richard wants to wed, questions his identity in Act 4, Scene 4: "Who dost thou mean shall be her king? . . . / What were I best to say? Her father's brother / Would be her lord? Or shall I say her uncle? / Or he that slew her brothers and her uncles? / Under what title shall I woo for thee . . . ?"; 143.

[14]Susan Wolf, "Ethics, Legal Ethics, and the Ethics of Law," in David Luban, ed., *The Good Lawyer*, (Totowa, N.J.: Rowman & Allanheld, 1984), 42, 43. Wolf believes that "the professional ideal of a lawyer most naturally is and . . . ought to be understood as an ideal with substantial moral content. In other words . . . being a good lawyer is more like being a good teacher than it is like being a good artist"; 43.

person who is really king or rabbi or teacher, self and role merge, no "natural person" is separable.

Wolf believes that many roles are more detachable than those of rabbi and teacher, but do they make visible a natural person behind them? Consider Jones, a member of the school board: this is one of her roles although certainly not the only one. Insofar as she is a parent, many of her decisions are those of a parent, but many other things enter even that role—her values and preferences, her abilities, her conception of being a parent. Thus the role of parent becomes intertwined with other aspects of her life. And when she votes on the school board she fulfills a community role that is also tied up with various aspects of her self and life. When does she act as a natural person? One answer is, always, for she shapes her role and it thus expresses who she is. Another answer is, hardly ever, since nearly anything of importance that she does reflects some role or other.

Look at how this works in detail. Jones votes at a school board meeting, a vote that reflects her beliefs about education and her purpose in being on the board: she ran, let us say, as a supporter of educational basics, which has been her stand as a citizen and a parent. These beliefs are not compartmentalized, however, for they contributed to her running for office and in turn influenced her constituency to vote for her. Should we call these the opinions of a "natural" person? No, since they reflect, among other things, her interests as a parent and a member of the community, both of them roles. But in that case it seems that her presence on the board and her actions there can't be separated from the rest of her life. Various roles and relationships combine in her personal beliefs, and all help to show who she is and why she voted the way she did. It is as *that* person of various roles and background, not as the natural-person-Jones, that she was elected, and as that person she votes. Her case now resembles the king's, where role and character cannot be separated even though the formal role requirements can be specified. Therefore Wolf's distinction is more complicated than it seems, the division between identifying roles and other kinds less clear cut. This raises the question whether, after a number of years in the job, even the waiter's role is sharply distinguishable from his identity.[15]

[15]Consider the identity of P. G. Wodehouse's Jeeves for instance, after long years of service to his employer.

V

Let us look at the concepts of role and self more generally. Lionel Trilling says of using the term "role" to talk of positions and functions that "the old histrionic meaning [of role] is present whether or not we let ourselves be aware of it, and it brings with it the idea that somewhere under all the roles there is Me, that poor old ultimate actuality, who, when all the roles have been played, would like to . . . settle down with his own original actual self."[16] Talking in terms of roles implies that a person must be separate from his role and otherwise could not have it. Having a role, like having a house, implies a relation between two things, a person and something she has; thus self and role can't be merged. A different actor might have played Othello tonight, and similarly my role, like my house or address, could belong to someone else. But speaking this way, we must have a clear idea of identity from which all such roles can be subtracted, a bare Me.

A person takes on a work or professional role, a person with a character and preferences who makes choices. But realistically she makes these choices from within a context in which she already has roles, some of which are not chosen. A person begins a working life but already has a role or position in her family, a name and a history, and a multitude of relations to others. She chooses this job instead of another or instead of none: does she do this from outside her roles? No, some roles were there and follow her. If we try to subtract her prior connections and their relation to her personality we become lost. Can we suppose that she might not have been her parents' child or might not have any relations to others at birth?[17] The question defies understanding.

We are drawn toward the conclusion that one's identity or real self cannot be a distinct Me somewhere under all the roles. It is more closely tied up with roles and relations than such separation allows, and some of them are connected with human generation itself. The original actual self eludes us.

[16] Lionel Trilling, *Sincerity and Authenticity* (Cambridge, Mass: Harvard University Press, 1972), 9–10. I owe this quotation to David Luban, *Lawyers and Justice* (Princeton, N.J.: Princeton University Press, 1989), 111.

[17] Van Laan interprets the tragedy of Romeo and Juliet in terms of such fundamental roles: the lovers "make the tragic error of believing that they can easily shed their familial roles in order to assume the leading parts" in an inappropriate romantic drama; *Role Playing in Shakespeare*, 37.

Against the tendency to separate the self from contingent relations, Aristotle held that a person *is* an amalgam of roles, that their number and complexity enhances one's self and makes existence more characteristically human. A man, he says, *is* all his important roles, the father of so-and-so, the husband of so-and-so, owner of such property, citizen of such city, participant in such military action, holder of office, and so on. Against Sartre, Aristotle would protest that roles are good and enriching features of our lives.

This view makes sense of such self-introductions as "I'm assistant to so-and-so at such-and-such," "I am Telemachus, son of Odysseus." Positions and family origins are the common means by which strangers make themselves known to each other, different ones invoked in different contexts.[18] It is also how we often identify third parties. Who is that person?—she is the person who does this, who is situated in these relations to others.[19] An "old ultimate actuality" without relations or background is much harder to talk about.

Relations and jobs are, as Aristotle held, indispensable for identifying people. Even the question, "Who is that woman in the red coat?" demands to place her in a context. Its answer will have the form, "She is the chief executive officer of . . . , the daughter of . . . , the author of . . . ," etc.; without some such reference, how could anyone answer? If one tries to leave out all references to positions and relations and tries to stay with the terminology of natural persons—for example "She is the woman who lives at 153 Walnut"—her identity remains obscure; she remains a mystery person.

[18] This concept bears striking similarity to what Sartre says about undertakings: "Man is no other than a series of undertakings . . . the sum, the organization, the set of relations that constitute these undertakings"; "Existentialism Is a Humanism," trans. Philip Mairet, in Walter Kaufmann, ed., *Existentialism from Dostoyevsky to Sartre* (New York: Meridian Books, 1957), 301. However, what Sartre means by undertakings (sometimes translated "projects") is something like ends to be strived for and for which one engages in actions. This is different from roles, though there is surely some overlapping—e.g., an entrepreneur starting a business has both an undertaking and a role in doing so.

[19] Van Laan comes to a similar conclusion about identity. For most characters, he writes, "identity [is not] some kind of unified personality . . . but rather the nexus of the various social roles that they are given to play." He explains: "I use 'nexus' to denote a connected group in which all elements of substantive if not equivalent impact and in which the various elements interact simultaneously"; *Role Playing in Shakespeare*, 26, 30, and see also 38. If I understand this, it means that identity is constituted by one's principal roles.

One source of difficulty here is the terminology of roles itself and the framework that it entails. Calling positions like teacher, manager, king, wife *roles* obscures the way a person brings his character to his position and the way one's position reflects and is reflected onto other aspects of one's life. Thus, Sartre's requirement that a person should be and act "as he really is" cannot exclude the demands of a person's commitments and obligations. But this means that there is no conflict between these and who he is. Commitments and the individual contributions of a person to his position are inseparable from the person himself. Bad faith is not so threatening in this view.

The relations and obligations that bind a person to others, together with the ways he handles these, belong to his identity. Even Thoreau, cut off from society and living in isolation at Walden, stood in important relations to the animals, to his bean field, his neighbors, to the nearby town, and even society in general.[20] His attitudes toward all these belong to his idea of how people, and how he in particular, should live. That way of living, with those convictions and attitudes and those relationships, *is* being Thoreau, you might say. Moreover his life at Walden undoubtedly changed and shaped him, contributed to who he was subsequently and to his subsequent roles and relations.

In the conceptual framework of roles, a roleless self seems necessary; but when we try to make it palpable we find an illusion, or better, a fantasy.[21]

VI

And yet people are detachable from some of what are called roles; they can leave or change jobs, for instance. And this detachability points back toward an underlying Me that continues the same. The baker who becomes an insurance salesman is the same person he was, though his identity as baker is gone. He *was* the baker, but changed his job—*his* job, which is to say the

[20] For instance Thoreau tells of his revulsion of eating the wild things around him: "I have found repeatedly . . . that I cannot fish without falling a little in self-respect. . . . With every year I am less of a fisherman"; *Walden and Civil Disobedience* (New York: Penguin, 1983), 261.

[21] To attempt to be a transcendant self without a role, David Luban says, is "romantic posturing," a mimicking of "the adolescent, standing at life's crossroads with ideals too high for the compromises of professional roles"; *Lawyers and Justice*, 115.

job of someone who can't be straightforwardly identified as a baker. There must be a continuing person, then, a detachable Me, who endured and whose job it was.

It's easy to mystify ourselves here. "The former director of the San Francisco symphony" helps identify a particular person. Is that past role part of his identity? He might instead have been the priest his father hoped he would be. Then would he be the same person he is now?[22] The "same" in what sense? He would be son of that same father, the one with that ambition, but he would not be the former director of the symphony. Then is he the same? Such puzzles of identity easily become a game whose premise is *either* the complete independence of a person from his roles *or* his complete identification with them. Neither is right.

Descartes conceived of the human self as a spirit independent of and different in kind from its physical body, and this idea fits naturally with a hard distinction between self and roles. It resembles the underlying Me Trilling speaks of. Such a distinction is also reflected in Montaigne's claim to have separated himself from his many roles—of mayor and judge, counselor, landlord, and writer. "We must play our part duly," he says, "but as the part of a borrowed character. Of the mask and appearance we must not make a real essence." There is a distance between person and role, he says, and he insists that "the mayor and Montaigne have always been two, with a very clear separation." They coexist without conflict: "I have been able to take part in public office without departing one nail's breadth from myself, and to give myself to others without taking myself from my self."[23] But in reality, even formalized roles may reach into the rest of one's life and Montaigne's boast is suspect. For instance,

[22] I manufacture this example. A real one is presented by Phyllis Morris in her exploration of the dramatic transformation of Malcolm X when he converted to the faith of Islam. At that point, she says, he saw his former self as a different person and "was a new person, in a sense"; *Sartre's Concept of a Person*, 81. But it is also true that the person he *became* cannot be separated either from his former self or the transformation.

[23] Montaigne, "Of husbanding your will," in *Complete Essays of Montaigne*, trans. Donald M. Frame (Stanford, Calif.: Stanford University Press, 1958), 773, 774. Montaigne also expressed some uneasiness about his detachment from these personae, saying, "I do not know how to involve myself so deeply and so entirely" as others do; 774. For a discussion of Montaigne's personal struggle with his roles and his sense of identity, see Frederick Rider, *The Selfhood of Montaigne* (Stanford, Calif.: Stanford University Press, 1973).

one top executive describes the kind of managers his company wants: "We want someone with breadth, with some interests outside the business, someone who is broad as a person. And this can be anything—the arts, sports, or both, in local politics, in Toastmasters, in Little League."[24] The qualifications wanted may make a separation such as Montaigne advises impossible; it may make the would-be manager reshape his personal life to fit the job.

The problems with Trilling's underlying Me and Montaigne's detachable self are deep. Even the newborn child has a set of relations to a family and community and therefore has (though it cannot actively play) the roles that these entail. Lacking some of these roles, would the child not be a different child? The question's sense is cloudy: *how* would the child be different? Criteria that are connected with ordinary questions about identity have no purchase here. We need more than the bare self if we are going to discuss identity.

In ordinary questions whether one person is the same as another, for instance whether the baker is the man in the blue hat, or this scholar is author of that book, "same person" is connected with definite criteria—name and family and other things among them—and the criteria will vary with the context in which the question is raised. Normally, given the context, we know how to answer. In our present discussion, however, identity is pressed into an abstract service where its normal grammar is untraceable and where its usual contexts are missing.[25] Thus, while the question "Would the waiter be the same person had he not been a waiter?" seems ordinary, it isn't. If we say that he *is* the onetime waiter, do we imply that he would be the same person had he *not* been? One has no idea how "the same person" is being used in this question. The understood criteria and their usual contexts have been left behind; the phrase is cut adrift from its grammatical moorings.

[24] Jackall, *Moral Mazes*, 58. The remark is quoted anonymously by Jackall, who uses pseudonyms for the managers and the companies he studied.

[25] See Lars Hertzberg, "Imagination and the Sense of Identity," in Raimond Gaita, ed., *Value and Understanding* (New York: Routledge, 1990), for a discussion of the relation of contexts to questions about identity.

VII

It is not easy to escape the framework of roles. Amelie Rorty writes that

> our idea of persons derives from two sources: one from the theater, the *dramatis personae* of the stage; the other has its origins in law. . . . A person's roles and his place in the narrative devolve from the choices that place him in a structural system, related to others. The person thus comes to stand behind his roles, to select them and to be judged by his choices and his capacities to act his personae in a total structure. . . . The idea of a person is the idea of a unified center of choice and action, the unit of legal and theological responsibility. Having chosen, a person acts, and so is actionable, liable. It is in the idea of action that the legal and the theatrical sources of the concept of person come together.[26]

"The person comes to stand behind" her roles—but that raises anew the problem of the mythical actual self. Rorty leaves ambiguous whether there was a self first or whether roles can give identity. What is important according to her is the actions, actions of choosing roles as well as performing in them; for her the connection between self and roles lies in action.[27] Thus she sees roles as a reflection of taste and preference and not as restricting who a person is or the roles one can choose. However, we have found on the contrary that roles include unchosen relationships, which, together with our abilities, handicaps, and limitations of circumstance, may tightly restrict our options. An actor is born with a talent and a taste for the stage; otherwise it would be pointless for him to choose that career. And that talent may be encouraged by the example of family members. How can we separate the particular self from all such relations, abilities, influence, and context? We cannot.

---

[26] Amelie Rorty, "A Literary Postscript: Characters, Persons, Selves, Individuals," in Rorty, ed., *The Identities of Persons* (Berkeley: University of California Press, 1976), 309.

[27] One may feel uneasy about using "acts" indifferently in both theatrical and professional contexts. For a lawyer may "act," i.e., play a part, in the courtroom, as distinguished from his "acting" as agent of his client. But I refrain in this context from discussing the ambiguity in depth. Rorty's view reminds one of John Locke's claim that "person" is a forensic term "appropriating actions and their merit, and so belongs only to intelligent agents capable of law"; *An Essay Concerning Human Understanding*, book II, ch. 27, sect. 6. By "capable of law," however, Locke meant capable of divine law, which includes humans who may not be governed by civil law. His point is that the concept of person is used to place responsibility and administer punishment.

Sociologist Ralph Linton addresses the tension between self and roles by invoking a kind of master role: "every individual has a series of roles deriving from the various patterns in which he participates and at the same time *a role*, general, which represents the sum total of these roles and determines what he does for his society and what he can expect from it." Linton seems to mean that the summary or master role governs the specific ones, and this connects a person to the society.[28] But is the master role expressive of the person within, in which case the old problems of the self rise again? Or can we have a master role with no possessor?

Even if we could identify a roleless self, what would we do with it, what point would there be to separating it? The person we want to hold responsible, or chide, or whose help we want to solicit, is always attached in one way or other to a context in which he has a particular place or role. He is already a politician, a thief, a doctor, union member, and so on. David Luban writes that "when we focus exclusively on the man-behind-the-social-mask, we are naturally led to impoverish our moral vocabulary."[29] We need more than that self, a thicker, three-dimensional person with relations and ties to others, if we are to treat a human as a moral entity.

VIII

Confusions about roles and identity are common in discussions of professions. For example, Gerald Postema writes that the profession of law "defines an *identity* for its occupant, a *self* awaits the person entering the role." The question he raises is "how does a person regard the self defined by the role . . . [and] come to terms with oneself in the role?"[30] Once roles and selves are separated, this question is pressing. At the same time, as we found, it is unanswerable.

[28] Ralph Linton, *The Study of Man* (New York: Appleton Century, 1936), 114. Sartre also speaks about a person being "the sum, the organization, the set of relations" that constitute his undertakings, as if this vocabulary suffices to represent a whole person; "Existentialism Is a Humanism," 301. But this doesn't appear consistent with his discussion of bad faith. Cf. Morris's discussion in *Sartre's Concept of a Person*, 54.

[29] Luban, *Lawyers and Justice*, 114–15.

[30] Gerald Postema, "Self-Image, Integrity, and Professional Responsibility," in Luban, ed., *The Good Lawyer*, 287.

We find that the terminology of roles shapes and bends our reasoning toward the theatrical model, but it is too spare for discourse about persons taken entire and their moral responsibilities. One problem is that this terminology is simply too spare for personal identity. As Hamlet can be acted by different actors, we are encouraged to think that anyone is replaceable while duties attach to a role impersonally. Thus, roles make people appear to be role-fillers who perform in a required way but whose actions are not personally theirs.

A second problem with the theatrical paradigm is that it makes jobs, with their obligations, seem too bounded and discrete, too complete and packaged. Obviously, the stage forms a world sharply marked off from the everyday one. But a person in a position has multiple relations, both within and without the work context, and all have their obligations. These obligations interconnect, compete, conflict restlessly, and require constant sorting out.[31] But in sorting out the choices, one is not helped by thinking of circumscribed and discrete roles, as if the choice were between systems and values. A larger framework is needed—and a more personal one.

A third problem with the language of roles and the theatrical paradigm is that dramatic roles are self-justifying in a way that work and professional roles are not. I mean that no moral justification is required for someone doing a brutal or wicked thing onstage. The role of an unscrupulous person belongs in and is part of an aesthetic work, and if anything justifies such action, the work itself does. After all, no one is harmed.

Thus, comparing a professional to an actor in a role encourages the exclusion of certain actions from moral criticism. Some

[31] The officer corps of the military appears to be an exception, according to Anthony Hartle. He speaks of a military "culture" with its own values, norms, and symbols, as well as "special guides to behavior in social situations." The officer corps has a "corporate structure," he says, which includes "not just the official bureaucracy but also societies, associations, schools, journals, customs, and traditions." As a result, "the professional world of the officer tends to encompass an unusually high proportion of his activities. He normally lives and works apart from the rest of society." Again: "Military professionals unquestionably have a strong sense of identity, reinforced by a certain alienation from the society they serve"; Hartle, *Moral Issues in Military Decision Making* (Lawrence: University Press of Kansas, 1989), 19–20, 15–16, 22. The packaging—and the distance it puts between the professional and the rest of society—makes such professions resemble the theatrical model but also makes them morally problematic.

things are required by the role, that is all. This attitude is found where people think in terms of roles. Robert Jackall, for example, tells how corporate managers he wished to interview showed uneasiness at moral language; they "urged me to avoid any mention of ethics or values altogether and concentrate instead on the 'decision-making process' where I could talk about 'trade-offs' and focus on the 'hard decisions between competing interests' that mark managerial work."[32] Role-thinking thus encourages a kind of insulation from moral scrutiny, after the theatrical model. Yet the reality is that while an actor who makes us shrink with horror might be praised for his good acting, the unscrupulous lawyer of politician or business manager is something else again.

A fourth and final problem: the accomplished actress in her roles shows little of her own character and personality, her real character. She one time acts a villainess and later a saint, now an ingenue and then an old woman, without any of these parts saying much about herself. Moreover, her parts may not affect her personal attitudes; in that way they are detachable. Outside the theater, by contrast, what someone does in her jobs and other roles may reveal a lot about her. And she in turn is informed by her position, educated and changed by it. This is another theme of the following chapters: that to ignore the connections between our various positions and relations leaves out a great deal that makes sense of our moral lives.

In defining the artificial person, Hobbes clearly had the theatrical model in mind, and the theatrical resonance is often heard in modern discussions. But the reference is unfortunate, for it frustrates both a clear view of such persons and our attempts to deal with them in moral terms. Therefore we will now consider artificial persons without this terminology.

[32] Jackall, *Moral Mazes*, 14.

FOUR

Fractured Autonomy

In general, where there is a significance for good or ill, agent action and consequence are connected together internally.

R. F. Holland, *Against Empiricism*

WE HAVE SEEN that problems stem from acting for others, yet the practice does not seem inherently wrong. How do the problems arise, and what conditions are needed to preserve responsibility? Can we have both artificial persons and individual responsibility in one social arrangement? These are the next questions we address.

I

Of something done by an artificial person, common sense wants to ask an elementary question: which person *really* acts—the author, the actor, or both? Clearly, both are involved. Then is the action both the agent's *and* the author's, a single action shared between them? If not, whose is it? In Hobbes's scheme this question is blocked, as it is in the simplest examples of agency. The sovereign's action *is* the action of the state and indistinguishable from it, the infant's action *is* his guardian's. Neither can act as "natural persons," they *must* be represented. However, differences between the various forms of artificial persons need to be kept in mind. While children, incompetents, nations, and investors of corporations can act only through a representative, adult and competent authors can usually act on their own. They have two alternative ways of doing many things, through others or by themselves—Hobbes would say they can act in either the fictional or real mode; it is a matter of choice. Such are the important cases for us here.

Being represented by someone seems untroublesome on its face. If I send a lawyer with power of attorney to arrange a contract, whatever he arranges is binding on me. The contract is *my* contract; I might as well have signed it myself. Put another way, since he commits me as I asked him, his action can be regarded as mine by extension. He helps me in something much as a long stick helps me get something out of reach. He is an instrument and involved in my action the way the stick is involved, no more. The analogy implies that the resulting action is mine, just as what I do using the stick is mine and not the stick's. The only difference is that, in using the stick, I act at a *physical* distance from what is done; in using a person, I act at a *personal* distance. Thus, if I authorize the lawyer to act only in ways that I am ready to be committed to, I can criticize his performance and the quality of representation if he fails, but his action is nonetheless mine, just as much as the sovereign's action is the people's.

Neat though it is, this answer is incomplete. We want to know, *morally speaking*, in what sense the lawyer's actions are mine and in what sense they are his. He acts for me; yet he consents to being my representative and willingly gives his cooperation. In this respect the servant too has some responsibility, for his cooperation is voluntary; and the lawyer is no servant— moreover, he is well paid for what he does. He must be involved somehow. And suppose that my lawyer acts deceitfully while negotiating for me, does something I would neither do nor authorize him to do. What I charged him to do, as I describe it, is perfectly honorable; the moral problem arises with how he accomplished it. Now who is responsible for his deceit? Both Hobbes and agency theory respond that I am.

Critical of the simple identification of agent with author, Oliver Wendell Holmes, Jr. argued that common sense would hold an author responsible only for what he commands. If "it be extended beyond that point it simply embodies the fiction" of responsibility which "sensible men" will be unwilling to sanction.[1] The invocation of common sense and sensible men here is an invocation of ordinary moral standards, but the appeal to

[1] Oliver Wendell Holmes, Jr., "Agency II," in Holmes, *Collected Legal Papers* (New York: Harcourt Brace & Co., 1920), 111–12. Remember that Holmes is a harsh critic of the law on agency, calling it "the resultant of a conflict between logic and good sense—the one striving to carry fictions out to consistent results, the other restraining and at last overcoming that effort when the results become too manifestly unjust"; 101.

moral common sense is not as simple as Holmes thinks, as closer scrutiny shows.

A variety of cases are possible: for instance, instructions are open to interpretation, as we have seen with the military. Thus, if someone gives the instruction to "get rid of" a person, it might in some circumstances be understood to mean to kill him. If asked to "bring something from the store" an agent may think he should steal it. Even in a familiar context there is often room for misunderstanding, for commands have a pervasive ambiguity and incompleteness, and that in turn generates ambiguity about who is responsible for whatever is done. Moral common sense cannot cut through this problem so easily.

Suppose we craft a simple solution. The author signs an affidavit claiming full and unconditional responsibility for her agent, whatever he does. The affidavit is properly signed and witnessed; it declares the author's responsibility and specifically releases the actor from culpability. Now, although it seems that it *should be* possible for the author to take responsibility for an actor's deed, even here responsibility is cloudy. For it is still the lawyer who deceived without being told to, and the fact that he did so as part of a job and in the name of the author doesn't free him entirely from responsibility. The affidavit can't so neatly exculpate him, even Holmes's "sensible person" would say, although the wrong would not have been done without her initial command.

One might object that although the author is not responsible directly, she is responsible indirectly, at least, for sending a person who would use unethical means, for employing a person of such character. If you ask someone to act in your name, you should be sure it's someone whose character you can trust: the missions of Sir Tristan and John Alden are nice cases in point. But in everyday situations where lawyers routinely represent others, it's difficult to fault an author for an actor's character unless the deficiency is flagrant and well known.[2]

Now suppose that deceiving is part of the job, that an agent is told to go and deceive someone—a competitor or an unsym-

---

[2] Holmes writes that "in torts it is sometimes said that the liability of the master is 'in effect for employing a careless servant.'" But, he objects, "this reason is shown to be unsound by the single fact that no amount of care in selection will exonerate the master"; "Agency I," in *Collected Legal Papers*, 54.

pathetic Congress, for example. Here responsibility stands differently. Having ordered the deception, the author must share responsibility for it. This echoes Holmes's condition of command. But still the author cannot take *full* responsibility for deceiving, just as she cannot take responsibility for the details of other actions. The actor is a free person, not a slave, and acts voluntarily; thus his action has to meet whatever moral conditions apply to voluntary action. Again, he cannot be exempted from responsibility.

The paradoxical fact emerging is that an author can *claim* responsibility for an action, explicitly *assume* responsibility for it, take legal action to relieve another of responsibility—*and* that these are not conclusive. Thus it appears that moral responsibility can't be so easily passed around, can't be held and transferred like a proxy, or treated as the legal fiction of agency and the artificial person require. And the interesting question is why, when both parties are amenable, this transfer of responsibility should *not* be possible.

II

If actor and author must share responsibility when an artificial person acts, can we divide that responsibility along some plausible lines? Could we suppose that the author who ordered the deception is not responsible for anything except giving the order, just that much? Then carrying it out would be the sole and full responsibility of the actor. If we are assuming that there is one action, a misdeed to which a certain punishment attaches— say, a twenty-year sentence—can we now divide it so that ten years of imprisonment is attributable to the author and ten to the actor; or could we give five to one and fifteen to the other?[3] To allocate a fraction to each, we must first weigh the contribution each made. But following this line, we depart from what Hobbes proposes and what agency law entails, namely, that there is only *one* action, not done in person by the author but nonetheless hers. Our procedure implies that there are two

[3] Peter French argues that "there is not a set amount of blame for every event," and thus clears the way for punishing *both* a corporation and an individual for the same action; *Collective and Corporate Responsibility* (New York: Columbia University Press, 1984), 9. I discuss this proposal further in Chapters 5 and 8.

distinct actions to be judged separately. Thus, instead of solving the problem by dividing responsibility, we differentiate two actions as if they had no claim to be one, which belies both the understanding of the parties and the theory that they acted under.

Thus the inference gains plausibility that artificial persons produce actions strikingly different from those in which the author makes a plan and carries it out alone. They bring about either a different *kind* of action or some *complex of actions* in place of a simple one. In either case Hobbes's claim that there are two ways of doing the same thing and the corollary that artificial persons' actions are fully attributable to the author are untenable. One cannot equate a deed done in person with something done in her name at a personal distance; they are not the same action.

It follows that using an artificial person is not, as we supposed, like using a stick to reach farther than the length of one's arm. It is not like accomplishing a given result in a different physical way, say, creating a lake by building a dam instead of digging a depression, where the actions done are comparable. An artificial person changes actions morally, and one reason this happens is that the responsibility associated with doing the deed oneself is not conserved. Even where there is shared responsibility, it is not shared the way a pie is: there may result greater total culpability with a two-party than with the one-party action. Or, as I will argue often happens, there may be less: responsibility tends to evaporate.

III

Let us reconsider the separation of what is done into two actions with two parties acting one after the other. The separation implies that the author is culpable only for his order, while the agent is culpable only for its execution. Such an analysis was proposed with respect to military actions by Nicholas Fotion and Gerard Elfstrom, who assert that "the necessity of war forces . . . [the] sharing of assigned responsibility across all ranks, where those with high rank take responsibility for ordering and those with low rank for actually doing whatever needs to be done."[4] However, the authors don't tell us how the sharing should be done, so let us make an effort in that direction.

Consider what kind of action the giving of an order is and how it counts morally. We need this information, as the judges at Nuremberg needed it to decide who was responsible for the war crimes. In one sense, giving an order is making a certain noise in appropriate circumstances, circumstances where it will be understood and perhaps acted on. But its being acted on is not part of giving the order, and thus not the commander's responsibility. On the other hand, where the order is executed and leads to something awful, how does one measure the moral significance of that noise-making?

In real examples many factors enter. The commander might not have any direct experience with the deed he orders, or he may be ignorant of the probable consequences, may even be shocked when they occur. Fotion and Elfstrom observe about the military that

from the point of view of those who give orders, what gets done becomes remote, so it becomes difficult for them to assess militarily and morally what is happening . . . [while] from the point of view of those doing the shooting, their sense of moral responsibility will often be no match for the levels of responsibility that are laid at their feet by their commanders and society.

Differences of experience and sophistication also cloud the assignment of responsibility. Against such obstacles, Fotion and Elfstrom strive for a military code of ethics that will "apply both to those who are and are not well trained to follow . . . edicts"; they wish to establish a clear route toward fastening responsibility.[5] But this project seems formidably difficult.

We face two temptations: on the one side, to regard an order as separate from the action that carries it out; on the other, to regard the order-and-action as one complex. The former means dividing a two-party action into two discrete actions, which, as we saw, helps us out of one difficulty but into another; for placement of responsibility is made too sharp and individual, the parts of the action unrealistically separated. And in the back-

---

[4] Nicholas Fotion and Gerard Elfstrom, *Military Ethics: Guidelines for Peace and War* (Boston: Routledge & Kegan Paul, 1986), 69.
[5] Ibid.

ground is the question what force a command has when given to a free agent. On the other side, if we suppose that a single action-complex is performed by two people, any placement of responsibility is simply obscure: imagine the captain and the corporal given a joint trial for a single deed! Can they, like Siamese twins, be one person here while for other purposes they are two? Fixing an appropriate punishment depends on a clear view of who did the deed, and what the deed was, but here a clear view is exactly what is missing.

The difficulties of dividing an action in two lead us back toward Hobbes's model of only one action with one author who is responsible *tout court*. In the military case this means that the superior is fully responsible for what his subordinate does under orders.[6] But we cannot ignore the fact that artificial persons exercise some choices about how to carry out an order, and for these the author should not be held responsible. But if not for these—the means to doing what is done—then how is she accountable for their effects? Either way of trying to make sense of responsibility here—that is, treating what was done as either a one-party or a two-party action—leads to puzzlement.

IV

Moral theory provides a key to this puzzling state of affairs, for its central motif or paradigm is an individual who first decides and then executes actions, does both himself. Autonomy, from the Greek *auto-nomos*, means making laws for oneself or acting as a self-legislating individual.[7] It means that a person commands herself to act and acts under her own direction. This kind

[6]In discussing the distance between orders and their execution, Dennis Thompson says that in government "those who are most distant from the action are often the most responsible for it. . . . Unlike citizens, those [high level] officials . . . confront the immediate effects firsthand, they hear about them in vivid detail"; *Political Ethics and Public Office* (Cambridge, Mass.: Harvard University Press, 1987), 20. Exactly that ignorance of citizens serves to condition responsibility, on my argument, and helps to make it impossible to place.

[7]The sense of autonomy here is different from that by which I called social atoms autonomous, in both *Equality and the Rights of Women* (Ithaca, N.Y.: Cornell University Press, 1980) and *The Grammar of Justice* (Ithaca, N.Y.: Cornell University Press, 1987). The autonomy of social atoms lies in their being unconnected to others and able to shape their lives independently of others. I argue throughout that such an idea is unrealistic, as well as pernicious, for political theory. Moral autonomy in contrast is compatible with a multitude of relations and obli-

of action characterizes her as a moral agent, and distinguishes her on the one hand from persons unable to reason and on the other from those unable to act as they wish.[8] For instance, drugs may cloud one's thinking, and coercion may interfere with carrying out one's plans. A person may sometimes act by mistake or involuntarily, but what she does deliberately, after settling the question whether to act and how, is fully her responsibility.[9] Thus, the paradigm shows us people who can be held responsible for virtually all their voluntary actions.

Under this paradigm it is theoretically impossible for one person to take responsibility for actions done by another. The possible exception is the slave, that root figure for the theory of agency, because the slave is not fully a person in law. But, in general, if deliberation and choice of action are not wedded to doing—which is to say, if the person who decides is not the one who acts—there is strong reason for arguing a person's nonresponsibility.[10] If this is so, it means that an artificial person cannot act fully and morally *by definition*. She cannot because she acts as another person's surrogate, and such action cannot be assimilated to the moral paradigm.

The model for moral theory, then, is the single action planned and executed by one person. Where p and only p does action a, it is possible to speak in a straightforward way of p's responsibility for a.

While a is a single undivided action in the paradigm, there is an important sense in which it has parts: p may decide to do something that, when the moment comes, she hesitates about

---

gations to others, some of which one has no choice about; I stress the importance of these in the present argument.

[8] Autonomy, or the self-governing of individuals over themselves, was a focus of Kant's moral theory, but the idea originates much earlier. Bernard Knox points out that Antigone was described as *autonomos* in Sophocles' play. And although the term had been applied primarily to a *polis* rather than to individuals, Knox argues, autonomy became one of the principal features of the Sophoclean hero; *The Heroic Temper* (Berkeley: University of California Press, 1964), 66–67.

[9] For such a formulation, see D. G. Brown, *Action* (Toronto: University of Toronto Press, 1968), esp. 111–13.

[10] D. G. Brown, for instance, writes that where the condition of choice is missing, "then *either* it is not action *or* it is action but meets one of the many conditions for non-responsibility"; ibid., 114. The counterargument that people may indeed be held responsible for what they are coerced to do is made in detail by Harry Frankfurt, *The Importance of What We Care About* (New York: Cambridge University Press, 1988), essays 1, 3, and 4 in particular.

and finally refuses to do. At the moment of taking action it may happen that her original choice takes on a different color and cast, that what seemed good reasons beforehand now fade as she confronts the plan's execution. Thus, her choice and her reasons do not determine the action completely. Acting has to meet a further test, the test that what is chosen is something the moral agent can actually bring herself to do when she faces the circumstances. Think, for example, of Raskolnikov in Dostoyevsky's *Crime and Punishment*. It is easy to imagine that after framing all his reasons (e.g., that the world would be a better place without old Alyona, the pawnbroker) and determining to murder her, when the time comes he cannot do it. He finds that the deed is impossible.

Such a reversal would not surprise us. It is not Raskolnikov's calculations about Alyona's place in the world that shock us. What shocks is that, after pondering and weighing and deciding, *he can do what his calculations point to*, can deliberately raise the ax and kill Alyona. Hesitation, doubt, change of mind, these are familiar to all of us. We all know occasions where reasoning pointed to an action, and yet, when we faced doing it, we had to reconsider. We hesitated, rethought the reasons, and then changed our minds. Such occurrences are part of human moral experience, part of the self-legislating life.

Distinguishing these aspects of action helps to show why the use of artificial persons muddies the usefulness of the paradigm. Raskolnikov's autonomy is clear and dramatic, for he acted alone and voluntarily and there were no mitigating circumstances. The action satisfies the paradigm. But where an agent enters the picture the paradigm gets fractured. One person deliberates but doesn't confront the reality of acting; while another person confronts the circumstances and acts, but hasn't made the choice. Thus, the author who chose might have changed his mind, and the one carrying out instructions might have chosen differently had he been permitted to.[11] As it is, neither has an autonomous person's view of the thing he partici-

---

[11] Holmes observes that the agent's ignorance of the reasons that support what he is ordered to do creates difficulties; the idea that we can "unite the knowledge of the principal with the statement of the agent in order to make the latter's act fraudulent" is a manifest absurdity; "Agency II," 108.

pates in, and neither has the control that an autonomous person is supposed to have. Therefore neither party can be said to have done the deed in the fullest and strictest sense. Consequently, in the paradigmatic sense neither is responsible for it. Even calling it some *one's* action sounds strange.

Cannot an action involving two participants be considered in the same terms as an action done by one?[12] The question is elusive. Two people may *effect* what one person could have done alone; in that sense their action can be substituted for what one person does. But from the moral side such substitution is unclear. Suppose that while Raskolnikov planned the murder, he hired someone to execute it according to his instructions. Consider one unplanned part of the murder, the appearance of the hapless Elizavyeta, younger sister to Alyona. Surprised at her entry, Raskolnikov kills her. If someone acts as Raskolnikov's surrogate, the murder of Elizavyeta cannot be put directly at Raskolnikov's door, yet had Raskolnikov not commissioned Alyona's death it would not have happened. The second murder is clearly the hireling's deed, an improvisation; and yet the orders don't tell him how to deal with this eventuality, he must deal with it somehow.

V

In actions of an artificial person, then, the author and the actor are each missing part of the paradigm. The actor is missing the process of reasoning and choice; the author is missing what Thomas Nagel calls the "moral phenomenology" of the action. By this he means the experience of actually doing the thing, one's felt response to the action he has reasoned about.[13] A person isn't morally culpable for accepting an argument whose conclusion is that he should do something, what Aristotle calls "practical reasoning." An action has to materialize. But as we

[12] The ancient Greek Andocides refers to a rule that where an agent is used, willing an act is equivalent to doing it with one's own hand; J. Walter Jones, *The Law and Legal Theory of the Greeks* (London: Oxford University Press, 1956), 266. Since use of agents was common in Athens, this is legal acknowledgment of the need to unify fractured actions.

[13] Thomas Nagel, *The View from Nowhere* (New York: Oxford University Press, 1986), 180–82.

saw, an apparently justified action may repel one at the moment of confrontation and force its abandonment. Revulsion at doing such a thing is therefore pertinent moral information.

In the paradigm case where only one person acts, a collision can occur between what Nagel calls the "objective judgment" that something should be done and the phenomenological aspect of doing it. He describes this example: A life will be saved if you twist a child's arm and make the child scream, which will force his grandmother to assist in saving a person whose life is in danger. Nagel argues that objectively it is justifiable to twist the child's arm, but he is deeply repelled by it. This creates a paradox for morality. *"Things* will be better, what *happens* will be better, if I twist the child's arm than if I do not. But I will have done something worse." To do the deed, Nagel says, he faces being guided by evil, for it is precisely hurting the child that he must intend—if the child is unhurt his project is futile. "But the essence of evil is that it should *repel* us. . . . That is what evil *means.* So when we aim at evil we are swimming head-on against the normative current." Yet the objective reasons remain strong and convincing: "The immediacy of the fact that you must try to produce evil as a subsidiary aim is phenomenologically important," Nagel says, "but why should it be morally important?" He confesses that he lacks a clear answer and concludes that "the human duality of perspective is too deep for us reasonably to hope to overcome it,"[14] at least in our present state of moral development.

One way to justify a morally offensive action is to refer to a larger scheme of ends and consequences. That strategy is often used to defend actions of lawyers: the purposes of the legal system itself are invoked, a system in which clients depend upon representation by someone speaking in their behalf. Acting in this system has its requirements, the argument goes, and the *Moral Code of Professional Responsibility* states that "the duty of a lawyer to his client and his duty to the legal system are the same: to represent his client zealously within the bounds of the law." There is no distinction between the two obligations. David Lu-

[14]Ibid., 180, 182, 183, 185.

ban calls this the "adversary system excuse" for doing what would otherwise be censurable.[15]

Using the institution to justify professional duties opens the question of how the adversary system itself is justified. Various defenses are offered—for instance, "that the way to get at the truth is [to engage in] a wholehearted dialectic of assertion and refutation." Of this Luban asks why we should think the truth gets presented in this process, for the arguments are framed by interested parties. The argument from truth "seems to take as a premise . . . that truth is served by self-interested rather than disinterested investigation, a chancy assumption." Another argument says that the system itself embodies our idea of justice. Luban responds that the system does not further justice but often impedes it, and *that* is its real point: "the primary end of the adversary system is not legal justice but the protection of accused individuals against the state or . . . the preservation of the proper relation between the state and its subjects."[16] The justification for the system is really political—the protection of individuals, innocent or not, from government prosecution. It has to do with the relation between a citizen and the government which means, Luban says, that it has nothing to do with justice or morals.

Perhaps the most appealing argument asserts a fundamental right of anyone to pursue his legal rights, morally legitimate or not, through the machinery of the bar and the courts. If lawyers had a duty to select only just causes, then who would represent clients whose causes appear objectionable but are nonetheless legally sound? The bar is precisely the framework in which in-

[15] *ABA Model Code of Professional Responsibility* (1974 Revision) EC 7–1; quoted in David Luban, "The Adversary System Excuse," in Luban, ed., *The Good Lawyer*, 89.

[16] Luban, "Adversary System Excuse," 94, 97, 92. Luban argues that in this respect criminal and civil law differ and that "criminal defense is an exceptional part of the legal system, one that aims at protection rather than justice"; ibid. Others might refer here to justice as procedural and claim that the adversary system *is* central to justice in that sense. Anthony Hartle gives a kind of political justification for the military, too, arguing that its mission is justified by the nation's perceived need for it, as if the public's preference were justification enough. But a perception needs to be *correct* to give good justification, and he does not provide such evidence in *Moral Issues in Military Decision Making* (Lawrence: University Press of Kansas, 1989), see p. 23.

terpretation of law goes on; it is a field of give and take under argumentative pressure. Suppose that all other lawyers have turned a client down and you are the last one available, would you not have a duty to represent her? This last-lawyer-in-town argument brings the moral and political issues down to the wire.

Responses to the argument vary widely. Murray Schwartz argues that a lawyer has no general duty to represent someone with a wrongful purpose, because "all persons are morally accountable for their behavior, including behavior that assists others to achieve their ends. . . . No lawyer need accept any client . . . ; accordingly, voluntary acceptance of a client carries with it moral accountability for means and ends employed in that representation." Lawyers are responsible both for the cases they accept and for the means they use to pursue them. They show their own mettle by their choices and "should reject on moral grounds the immoral though lawful cause of a client." Yet, despite the appearance of inconsistency, Schwartz declines to forfeit the last-lawyer-in-town demand. He says that "a legal system is subject to moral criticism if it permits legal rights in some instances to go unrepresented in civil litigation because all lawyers refuse the representation on moral grounds." [17]

The problem of a right to legal representation invites criticism of the legal institution itself. Charles Wolfram holds that the right to representation cannot override moral objection, that "legal representation seems without significance apart from the use to which it is put." Thus, if all lawyers decline to accept a given client and "uniformity of moral judgments produces a de facto kind of extralegal social control, so long as the 'shunning' is not itself unlawful, then it would seem that it is morally justified." The system doesn't owe a right to be represented to all claimants. "I do not agree that a legal system should be accounted unjust if it leaves unrepresented [a] particular litigant whom no lawyer will represent because of moral objections." [18]

[17] Murray Schwartz, "The Zeal of the Civil Advocate," in Luban, ed., *The Good Lawyer*, 151, 152, 168. Schwartz resolves the conflict by proposing a system of compulsory assignment of representation for a case all lawyers have refused. This system has the double advantage of saving the lawyer from moral censure while at the same time providing representation, but it also sacrifices autonomy on the lawyer's side.
[18] Charles Wolfram, "A Lawyer's Duty to Represent Clients, Repugnant and Otherwise," in Luban, ed., *The Good Lawyer*, 233, 227.

Wolfram puts morality squarely in the middle of the debate, while on the other side, the American Bar Association code specifies that a lawyer should not pass judgment on a client's purposes. A lawyer ought to show partiality for the client and pursue his cause the best she can.[19] The code says nothing about the relation of this obligation to justice.

An important difference between lawyers and soldiers, on the one hand, and waiters, salesman and servants, on the other, is that the former deal regularly with morally charged matters. As Richard Wasserstrom notes, common opinion is that "a lawyer can appropriately . . . [assist] a wealthy, spiteful landlord to evict a needy tenant on a 'technicality'. Were someone else to [do so] . . . criticism might be appropriate."[20] Thus, where an action is morally questionable, a lawyer may be in a unique position to facilitate or frustrate it. Military personnel in wartime also deal continually with moral issues. This is why the behavior of these professionals is so in need of scrutiny.

Sometimes, seeing the bizarre outcome of a legal case, one says with a sigh, "that's how the system works," as if the system were mechanical and beyond human control, and this image fits with the terminology of roles pre-cut for a person to fill. If the poor tenant is evicted by his landlord through a perfectly legal action pursued by a perfectly correct and professional lawyer, how can this be wrong? But if it is not wrong, then why is it reprehensible for the landlord to throw the tenant out *without* the law and the lawyer? Why is it plain wrong for a client to refuse to repay a long-standing debt while he can get the same result legally through a lawyer? Does the game make the difference, does the lawyer's participation in it? Something strange happens to our reasoning here.

The underlying problem is that the institutional justification casts the issue in terms of roles, whose requirements defy straightforward moral evaluation. Within the institution, actions are shielded from such a critical light. This alone makes the justification morally suspect.

---

[19] A vigorous defense of this attitude is made by Monroe Freedman, "Professional Responsibility of the Criminal Defense Lawyer: The Three Hardest Questions," *Michigan Law Review* 64 (1966).

[20] Richard Wasserstrom, "Roles and Morality," in Luban, ed., *The Good Lawyer*, 27.

VI

Let us return to Nagel's case of sounding an alarm by causing a child to cry in pain. Sometimes one fails to act on a decision because of its difficulty or danger, or because of one's fear or disinclination.[21] Now, in this case the calculation of benefits shows a large balance of good results over bad if the child is hurt, and such calculation is absolute, not conditional on how a person sees the situation, how he feels faced with the abhorrent action that the calculation requires. Thus, how can Nagel's reluctance to act be distinguished from weakness of will?

To describe Nagel's repulsion and hesitation here as weakness of will supposes that advance reasoning can generally be trusted as a final moral guide. But this assumption is false, and its falsity is shown in both Nagel's and Raskolnikov's cases. Morality has to do with acting palpably in a three-dimensional world, not with abstract arguments using general principles.[22] It involves living with the flesh-and-blood immediacy of what one does, not only its description and subsumption under rules; and it means subsequently living with oneself as the person who did that thing.

How can moral theory account for the importance of the phenomenological side of moral action? The answer lies in an expanded account of moral understanding, one that recognizes that doing a thing in person, having personal contact with its execution, informs us in a way that general reasons do not. Such understanding complements arguments and shows an action in a different light, a light that is nonetheless relevant for moral criticism. Sometimes the difficulty of doing an action is foreseeable: one may say of an action that he considers well justified, "But I could never do it."

[21] Weakness of will (*akrasia*) is a central idea in Aristotle's ethical theory. He argues that while knowledge of what is right is essential, it isn't enough, since a person may be too weak to do what he knows he should.

[22] Peter Winch broadly attacks the idea that moral action and judgment are matters of applying general rules, and even that what is right for one person is right for another; "The Universalizability of Moral Judgments," in *Ethics and Action* (London: Routledge & Kegan Paul, 1972). I do not go that far. Luban scoffs at the idea of general moral calculations: "deliberating-by-number bears precisely the same relation to genuine practical reasoning that painting-by-number bears to art"; *Lawyers and Justice* (Princeton, N.J.: Princeton University Press, 1989), 136.

Such an example occurs in *Crime and Punishment*. Before the murder Raskolnikov overhears a student in casual conversation with an officer, who advances reasons for murdering the old pawnbroker. They are reasons precisely like those Raskolnikov invokes. But when the officer asks, "Would you kill the old woman *yourself?*" the student responds, "Of course not! I was only arguing the justice of it. . . . It's nothing to do with me." The officer objects, "But I think, if you would not do it yourself, there's no justice about it." He thinks that the student cannot have been serious in supporting the action if he is unready to commit himself to it. But I am arguing that this view is too narrow.[23]

Both considerations, ratiocination on one side and moral revulsion on the other, are real and legitimate criteria for evaluating actions morally. Our reluctance to do something, our repulsion at the brink of acting, does not show either that the reasoning is wrong or that we are weak of will. Instead, it may mean that we give greater weight to the deed's moral offensiveness than to other factors. It is too evil, to use Nagel's term; we cannot do it or live with ourselves if we do.

To act deliberately is a central idea for morality and this means more than just deliberating and deciding about an action that is then mechanical. It includes personal engagement with the circumstances, personally using instruments, and then observing the effects. It includes viewing oneself as the agent, an autonomous agent, aware of one's past experience and judgments. It rightly involves the question: What would I say if someone else were doing this? As a moral legislator one must be able to capture such a view of one's deeds.

If an action is morally sound, its being hard to do can bring satisfaction when one does it. But its moral offensiveness casts a shadow on such soundness that any serious agent should heed.[24]

[23] Fyodor Dostoyevski, *Crime and Punishment*, trans. Constance Garnett (New York: Macmillan, 1927), 61. The gap between what ought to be done, taken abstractly, and what one is justified in doing is discussed in chaps. 6 and 7 of *The Grammar of Justice*.

[24] Also see Gerald Postema on the importance in the law of a "willingness to identify with the consequences of one's action"; "Moral Responsibility in Professional Ethics," *New York University Law Review* 55, 1 (Apr. 1980): 78.

The issue of fractured action stands like this. On the one side, an agent does what he is told, he deals with the practical situation and relies on the judgment of others, though perhaps with misgivings. On the other side, an author sees the ends she wants to gain and how to secure them, but is insulated from the action. Yet with such insulation I ask if she can really know what she decided on, can fully grasp what action she chose. Would she herself have done what was done? If not, then her ignorance excuses her, in part at least, as for complementary reasons the agent's ignorance excuses him. This explains why responsibility seems to evaporate.

Revulsion at an action may have different significations. For instance, a young person training as a mortician might feel revulsion at what he is being taught to do, yet his choice to be a mortician does not merit moral criticism. A doctor learning to amputate a limb must feel terrible pangs of regret, must overcome revulsion at what she does. In such cases moral strength may mean mastering reluctance, overcoming one's revulsion, and keeping one's focus on the final benefits.

But these cases of overcoming revulsion should not be confused with the case where revulsion is moral and should be heeded. The point can be made with another example. Becoming inured to horrific actions was required of Nazi doctors in the concentration camps. Many became sick when told to make the "selections," the decisions about who should die and who should live. They were told, "That will pass. It happens to everyone."[25] In time most of them did get used to the job. How is this different from the doctor "getting used to" amputations?

While they bear similarities to Nagel's case, the Nazi doctors are very far from the doctor amputating a limb. Revulsion at having to perform an amputation is expected and natural because—beyond the difficulties of the physical act—the *need* to do it is regrettable; one does repellent things that are justified in the same way one does unpleasant chores. But these actions are not *morally* repellent nor do they cause the kind of revulsion that sickened the Nazi doctors. However repellent to our emotions, to our sympathy with others and our wish to make life better

[25] Robert Jay Lifton, *The Nazi Doctors* (New York: Basic Books, 1986), 308.

rather than worse for them, amputation is not an evil. Thus the distinction between moral and nonmoral offensiveness is not so difficult to draw.

I am arguing that moral revulsion is particularly relevant to artificial persons. Robert Graves relates an incident from World War I, where he was an officer. "I saw a German, about seven hundred yards away . . . taking a bath. . . . I disliked the idea of shooting a naked man, so I handed the rifle to the sergeant with me. 'Here, take this. You're a better shot than I am.' He got him; but I had not stayed to watch." [26] Graves was unable to shoot the naked and defenseless German, though he never doubted that Germans should be killed. He was persuaded he should do something that morally repelled him and finally could not do. Ordering a subordinate to shoot the German freed him from the conflict between his reason and his moral sensibilities. He could satisfy them both. The story thus shows the tension that can exist between what one believes to be right and the actions that belief points to—and the way that using an agent resolves it. Graves's resolution of the tension was in a sense cowardly, both because he failed to confront the conflict personally and because he implicated someone else in what he found morally repugnant.

We sympathize with someone who shrinks from killing a defenseless person and *cannot do it*, even though in the abstract the killing seems right and justified. We sympathize with the sensitive Graves, but the problem remains. His use of the subordinate, like the use of agents in general, worked to sanitize the action phenomenologically.[27] He protected himself from one kind of moral callousness but was guilty of another.

VIII

Involving ourselves personally in actions has crucial importance for moral education and development. The experience of carry-

[26] Robert Graves, *Good-bye to All That*, rev. ed., (Garden City, New York: Doubleday, 1957), 132.

[27] One might defend Graves by arguing that his revulsion at shooting the naked German was *aesthetic* and not moral. (It is unclear to me whether Graves would offer this excuse; he would concede that war necessarily involves people in many barbaric and morally awful things.) The same defense could be made of the protesting Nazi doctors. But the answer to this is that *refusing*, being *unable*

ing out our plans provides feedback, both about what our reasoning leads to and about ourselves—our sensibilities and tolerance, moral and other. When we are surprised to find we cannot perform an apparently justified action, this knowledge affects both our future reasoning and our self-understanding. Finding for ourselves what is tolerable and what is not is also learning about the limitations of abstract ratiocination.

Imagine that from childhood a person were only allowed to (or only able to) give orders and could never follow through and execute a plan himself. How does he view the actions that his decisions lead to? Only from the side of the reasons for and against. The child never experiences an action, or envisions it as something personal to him, as something *he does*. Lacking this, does he understand the actions really? And does he understand what it is to be a moral agent? He is an armchair moralist who misses the moral phenomenology of engagement and the self-knowledge that engagement brings with it. This means that his moral understanding and judgment of others, as well as of himself, is deficient. Unlike the student in the café, he does not worry about being morally unable to do what looks fine on paper or the possibility of a moral gap between reasoning and engagement. These things have no importance for him.

Adm. James Stockdale, celebrated as a war hero, has observed that "good judgment is based on experience, but . . . good experience is based on bad judgment."[28] We need to make mistakes, he says. My argument is that some mistakes can only be seen in personal encounter with circumstances, circumstances we first see abstractly and from a distance.

The Japanese military organization shows a different aspect of the connection between unified, unfractured action and moral responsibility. One Japanese scholar says that in World

to fire, does help exempt Graves from having done something morally abhorrent and thus proves his moral sensitivity; we sympathize with his response. Moreover, revulsion, sometimes deep and aesthetically terrible, is the right response to wrong and injustice. Calling it "aesthetic" does not remove its moral significance but only points to the way morals and feelings and emotions are intertwined.

[28] James Stockdale, *A Vietnam Experience* (Stanford, Calif.: Hoover Press, 1984), 20. His argument aims to cast a shadow on the separation of non-military order-givers and military order-executors, where the former have little or no firsthand experience with execution.

War II Japanese military personnel "did not regard themselves as active regulators but as men who were . . . being regulated by rules created elsewhere." Thus "in the absence of any free, subjective awareness, the individual's actions are not circumscribed by the dictates of conscience; instead he is regulated by the existence of people in a higher class." Every political person and military officer, even those high in the chain of command, saw themselves as passive agents of others. In the face of this, the American war crimes court finally admitted that "it has been impossible to find any individuals or groups that are conscious of having started the war." The war "did not result from any careful analysis of the world situation or from any study of comparative productive capacities and internal conditions."[29] It came about without *any* conscious intention. The court drew this frustrating conclusion: "Rather than to establish an agreement or common plan or conspiracy . . . the evidence [at the trials] definitely reveals the absence of leadership or of a centralized group committed to a common design or purpose of any kind."[30]

Actions in the Japanese context were not the expressions of anyone's individual decisions, although they *were* always seen as someone else's. "Where important matters of national policy were concerned, [the leaders] were not faithful to their own beliefs but repressed them as being 'personal emotions', choosing instead to adapt themselves to their environment; and this they made into their morality."[31]

A similar dispersion of responsibility is found in Japanese businesses and is embodied in the practice of *ringi*, a complex procedure of collective decision making that involves passing suggestions around and having each person, including junior and subordinate personnel, either approve proposals or suggest alternatives. A decision gradually comes about, evolves by a

[29] Masao Maruyama, *Thought and Behaviour in Modern Japanese Politics* (London: Oxford University Press, 1963), 16–17. Maruyama also notes that the leaders did not think of the war as having been started by Japan but as having arisen unavoidably. Unlike the Germans, he writes, "our own wartime leaders . . . were ultimately taken in by the slogans that they themselves had concocted, and as a result their view of reality was hopelessly obfuscated"; 95.

[30] *International Military Tribunal for the Far East, Proceedings*, No. 386 (1948), 423–889, cited in Maruyama, *Thought and Behaviour*, 86.

[31] Maruyama, *Thought and Behaviour*, 105.

kind of natural seasoning process.[32] In diffusing decision making over a whole structure, the system quiets anxiety about having individual responsibility, since any particular decision could be said to have had no individual author. It was taken by everybody. Or by no one.

The loss of responsibility in actions of artificial persons is traceable to their departure from the moral paradigm of a single person who both decides and acts. Representative practices vitiate these conditions and thus also the criteria for identifiable responsibility. This means that the shape of institutions and practices influences whether actions are done by individuals or simply "come about" and raises the suspicion that, by influencing the notion of responsibility, institutions may also influence what it means to be a person.

[32] Rodney Clark, *The Japanese Company* (New Haven, Conn.: Yale University Press, 1979), 127–28. Also see William Brown, "Japanese Management: The Cultural Background," in T. S. Lebra and W. P. Lebra, eds., *Japanese Culture and Behavior* (Honolulu: University of Hawaii Press, 1974), 180–82.

Corporate Persons

One of the weightiest objections to a plurality in the executive . . . is that it tends to conceal faults and destroy responsibility.
Alexander Hamilton, *The Federalist Papers*, No. 60.

SINCE ARTIFICIAL persons can be compound as well as individual, we need to consider the problems of multiple agents. I mean by "corporate" persons not only corporations but any agent composed of a number of people—boards, councils, senates, committees. All these have in common with other artificial persons that their function is to represent.

Hobbes noted that corporate persons lack some of the advantages of single spokesmen. For instance, a parliament lacks the advantages of a sovereign who can decide a policy and effect it without delay and debate. It is more efficient to have a single voice or decision maker. It is also morally simpler, as we shall see, for by complicating the question of agency, corporate action raises further obstacles to locating responsibility.

I

How do corporate actions differ from individual ones? Are composite actions reducible to those of individuals, or are they of a special kind, having a peculiar kind of agent?[1]

Calling a corporation a person extends the meaning of "per-

---

[1] For an argument that composite actions *are* reducible to individual ones, see J. W. N. Watkins's "principle of methodological individualism"; "Ideal Types and Historical Explanation," in H. Feigl and M. Broadbeck, eds., *Readings in the Philosophy of Science* (New York: Appleton-Century-Crofts, 1953), 729. Peter French argues against this principle in *Collective and Corporate Responsibility* (New York: Columbia University Press, 1984). I also discuss this below in section II.

son" and invokes a metaphor that many legal scholars find unproblematic. Legal theorist Hans Kelsen, for example, writes that "the concept of . . . person means nothing but the personification of a complex of legal norms. Man . . . is only the element which constitutes the unity in the plurality of these norms."[2] Person or man is a legal conception, he says, a locus of norms. Thus calling corporations persons only means that the norms that apply to humans apply to them. Others, however, find the fiction puzzling. John Chipman Gray asks, "Is the corporation . . . a real thing, or only a . . . fictitious entity? If it is a fictitious entity, we have a double fiction; first by fiction we create an entity, and then by a second fiction we attribute to it the wills of individual men." We create a fictional unity and then make it fictionally a *person*. Gray concludes that a corporation can be a person only in the sense that a horse or a ship can be; and a ship is a person only in the sense that the state recognizes it as the subject of rights.[3] Nothing more can be made of talking about a corporate person; the fiction is slender.

Hobbes's account makes more sense of the arrangement. Corporations represent individual stockholders and, as artificial persons, act in stockholders' names and "personate" them. Like other agents they are instruments through which people can do what they couldn't do otherwise. Hiring a lawyer gives one access to expertise in legal tactics, having a government allows one to have laws, having a military force provides one with capabilities for war. A corporation allows one to own (part of) a company and participate in its activities, and its representative organs allow stockholders to participate in many activities that would be impossible otherwise. Thus a corporation is analogous to the state: both perform in the name of a collection of people actions that could not otherwise be performed.

Congress is an instrument for governing, and the military is a communal instrument of war; then it may seem plausible that corporations are instruments for making money. On this view, they serve stockholders by returning a profit; that is their mission. One writer expresses this by saying that "the corporation

[2] Hans Kelsen, *General Theory of Law and State*, trans. Anders Wedberg (New York: Russell & Russell, 1961), 95.

[3] John Chipman Gray, *The Nature and Sources of the Law*, 2nd ed. (New York: Macmillan, 1931), 52, 56.

is an intermediary between its owners—the stockholders—and the resources other than the stockholders' capital, the services of which it purchases."[4] The image is mechanical. A corporate person takes investors' resources, makes use of them, and provides the investors with profits the way a mill takes grain and returns flour. Like lawyering and soldiering, a corporation's purpose can therefore be viewed as highly specialized and narrowly defined. As one economist puts it, "the function of business is to produce sustained high-level profits."[5]

Understood as devices for making money, corporations more closely resemble machines than human beings. Humans have no such limited "purpose," and their connections with others include many that are (financially) unprofitable and even taxing. The question must be addressed, then, in what sense are we to understand the fictional personhood of such entities? An artificial person is by definition impersonal, depersonalized. In what sense can corporations be considered persons *beyond* this limited artificial person sense? Are they able to take social and moral responsibilities seriously or concern themselves with the dimensions of moral choice? And if not, isn't it implausible to call them persons, even in the sense of a "unity of norms"? In short, how can corporations take their place beside humans in a community as anything other than amoral beings who live side by side with non-fictional, morally responsible persons?

II

Peter French takes corporate persons seriously and argues for their having a morally significant place alongside other mem-

[4]Milton and Rose Friedman, *Free to Choose* (New York: Avon, 1979), 12. Thomas Donaldson refers to this as the "Structural Restraint" view, which "emphasizes the fact that corporations are controlled by their very structures and are thus frequently incapable of exercising moral freedom"; *Corporations and Morality* (Englewood Cliffs, N.J.: Prentice-Hall, 1982), 23.

[5]Theodore Levitt, "The Dangers of Social Responsibility," in Thomas Beauchamp and Norman Bowie, eds., *Ethical Theory and Business* (Chicago: University of Chicago Press, 1979), 138; orig. pub. *Harvard Business Review*, Sept.–Oct. 1958. This view can be contrasted with the Japanese attitude that "service to society is laudable, but profit as an end in itself is suspect if not despicable," as articulated by an official of Matsushita who describes profit as "the appreciation of society, the reward to Matsushita for what it has done"; Rodney Clark, *The Japanese Company* (New Haven, Conn.: Yale University Press, 1979), 137.

bers of society. This requires a different idea of corporations and a different idea of what they are for. French offers this view:

Corporations are not founded, do not come into existence, to make money or to make a reasonable profit for investors. . . . Corporations make automobiles, airplanes. . . . Obviously they do so in order to make a profit, but with respect to the corporate personality and image, the factors that unify the corporate enterprise, the making of money especially for shareholders, is secondary. If the primary object of corporate enterprise were to make a profit, then there would be precious little to distinguish one corporation from another.[6]

Since the energy of a company is first of all dedicated to making a product or providing a service, this and not money making is what distinguishes its "personality." French likens the corporation's function to the military's role of defense or the law's role of dealing with complaints about justice. Businesses and professions have functions in the society as clear as those of gardener and carpenter and can be compared to these. But it isn't their functions that make the butcher and carpenter persons; something more is needed.

Plato once compared medicine and government in terms of their functions and argued that "the craft of medicine does not seek its own advantage but that of the body." In fact, "no physician . . . in so far as he is a physician, seeks or orders what is advantageous to himself. . . . He is a ruler over bodies and not a money maker."[7] Making money isn't the point of medicine any more than getting power and advantage is the point of governing.

But French's argument is unlike this. For Plato introduces the idea of responsibility into the very ground of medicine; the doctor seeks the advantage of someone else's physical health, the shepherd is charged with the welfare of his flock, and the ruler is charged with the well-being of his subjects. Each function is grounded in responsible relations with other creatures. Moral grounding does not come into French's characterization of the

---

[6]French, *Collective and Corporate Responsibility*, 102. It *is* curious to consider money making as a defining function of a corporation. The federal mint *makes money*; that is its function. But it isn't the function of tire and soft drink companies or hotels.

[7]*Republic*, trans. Paul Shorey, *The Collected Dialogues of Plato*, ed. E. Hamilton and H. Cairns (Princeton, N.J.: Princeton University Press, 1961), I, 340b–342d.

corporate function, though it enters his argument later, as we shall see.

As humans have personalities, French attributes distinctive personalities to corporations, and he claims that its personality is essential to a corporation's life. "The corporate personality . . . is . . . an invention, but its growth and development, its integration into the lives of the employees, and its perpetuation" show a resemblance to human beings. Therefore such entities should be taken seriously as persons, not just legally but morally.[8]

Look closer at this. "Metaphysical personhood," French says, "depends on the possibility of describing an event as an intentional action," an action done by a purposeful agent. Thus, the corporation per se needs to have intentions in acting, not simply the intentions of people in it, but its distinctive corporate ones. "What needs to be shown . . . is that there is sense in saying that corporations and not just the people who work in them have reasons for doing what they do."[9]

Corporate actions are not reducible to the actions of individuals, although individuals participate essentially in them: that is French's position. Similarly Hans Kelsen writes that the point of a corporation is to treat a collection of persons as a unity, "a person having rights and duties distinct from those of the individuals composing it, . . . [which] rights and duties are . . . created by acts of the organs of the corporation."[10] The corporation has its own rights and duties, which are not reducible to those of people in them.

But French's position goes further: a corporation has its own *intentions*, he argues, and can decide and act autonomously.[11] What assures this "metaphysical personhood" is its having a corporate internal decision (CID) structure, a structure of procedures and a line of authority for decisions that can be attributed

[8] French, *Collective and Corporate Responsibility*, 105. According to Gilbert Geis, the idea of *corporate* crime is not recognized in Europe, Asia, or the Soviet bloc countries. Yet in these contexts there is a literature on corruption and white-collar crime; "Criminological Perspectives on Corporate Regulation," in Brent Fisse and Peter French, eds., *Corrigible Corporations and Unruly Law* (San Antonio, Tex.: Trinity University Press, 1985), 68.

[9] French, *Collective and Corporate Responsibility*, 40.

[10] Kelsen, *General Theory*, 96.

[11] For an interesting discussion of the corporation as a moral agent and a criticism of French's thesis, see John Ladd, "Corporate Mythology and Individual Responsibility," *International Journal of Applied Philosophy* 2, 1 (Spring 1984).

to *it* in the way other decisions are attributable to humans. In sum, its structure establishes the corporation's personhood and allows it to take a place next to human members of the community.

By fleshing out the corporate fictional person, French makes it appear less fictional, more real and morally plausible, than it would seem otherwise. For instance, as humans have models of persons they would like to resemble, French says that "there surely are corporate ideal models as well." And these corporate images, like a person's moral aspirations, reflect moral character. Thus corporate image, which involves a corporation's reputation for good or bad deeds, now resembles character. "Public relations and advertising departments . . . play focal roles in every corporation's attempt to establish and nurture its social standing and its exemplary image in the community." [12]

In some ways corporations *are* like persons, for they participate in many practical transactions—buying, selling, contracting, and doing numerous other things that humans do. But, as Thomas Donaldson observes, "the mere fact that corporations share characteristics with human persons is inadequate to establish moral agency, since they also fail in this regard," and lack much that goes with being a human agent. They "do not feel pain, remorse, or pleasure; they are not descended from human parents and they enjoy both limited financial liability . . . and unlimited longevity." [13] Thus, comparing a corporation with a professional person likens it to only one side, the professional side, of a three-dimensional figure. But if people could be reduced to one function like this, we wouldn't have the troubles we do with obligations of multiple relationships. This move is akin to the one-dimensional analysis in terms of roles. The crucial issue is this: where do complex organizations and corporations fit into the social and moral world, a world whose other members are multifaceted humans?

---

[12] Peter French, "Publicity and the Control of Corporate Conduct," in Fisse and French, eds., *Corrigible Corporations*, 165.

[13] Donaldson, *Corporations and Morality*, 20. When one thinks of the life of a human, it is helpful to remember the variety of what Wittgenstein calls "language games," games of command and obedience, question and answer, games of expressing feelings and reacting to their expression, fantasizing, telling dreams, joking, etc. Viewed in this light, it is clear that corporations are excluded from much that characterizes humans' use of language and thus from their "form of life."

Another problem: in stressing the analogies with human beings, French suppresses the artificial person aspect of the corporation, that is, its function to represent stockholders. French would have a corporation resemble a human that acts and speaks for itself, but this means bypassing its artificial-person aspect, which is both a corporation's raison d'être and one source of its moral difficulties.

A last problem for French's account concerns punishment. Corporations can offend, can act to cause injury and deaths, but cannot go to jail; and punishment of a fine shows up as an expense on the corporate balance sheet.[14] This constitutes an obvious objection to their personhood. French answers that, instead of fining corporations, we should punish them by public shaming. Corporate self-respect is important, he believes: "Little success has ever been gained by a corporation with a bad reputation." He calls shaming the "Hester Prynne sanction," after the scarlet letter Hester was forced to wear for her adultery. How would shaming work? A corporation could be sentenced to commit part of its advertising budget to publicizing its misdeeds. In conjunction it could be sentenced to community service, to support of community projects. This might get corporations into the right habits, he argues; "a community service sentence could start a corporation on the path to virtue."[15] It amounts to corporate character development.

In stressing the importance of a good corporate image, French ignores an ancient distinction between having a good reputation and being virtuous. Anyone would be glad for a good reputation and its rewards, Glaucon argues in the *Republic*, especially if he could do what he pleased under its protection. That was part of the Gyges story: his invisibility protected him from being charged with his misdeeds. On the other side, being virtuous is not guaranteed to be either widely known or advantageous. In emphasizing the mission of a company's public relations depart-

[14] French thinks that fines have an important place in corporate punishment, even where the harms aren't monetary. He cites "the old Anglo-Saxon notion of *wergeld* utilized in settling wrongful death suits" to argue that human life has a price; "Publicity," 160. But this custom, and its connection with retribution, is now widely thought barbaric. That human life is not something with a simple monetary value, not even a high one, argues against the conception of *wergeld*. Otherwise murder would be all right so long as the price for the life is paid.

[15] French, *Collective and Corporate Responsibility*, 195. French, "Publicity," 170.

ment and the commercial importance of a good image, French keeps his argument in the amoral realm where only the appearance of character counts. And insofar as reputation may be connected with profits, this proposal leaves the issue of punishment where it was. Success in shady deals is something that a corporation may thrive on financially, and corporate citizens may, even in French's picture, resemble con men more than upright citizens. As community members, they may be among the most unscrupulous, wily, and difficult to deal with.

The problems of individual responsibility that characterize other artificial persons are at work when it comes to locating responsibility for corporate misdeeds. French suggests holding *both* the corporation *and* some individuals in it responsible for the same action.[16] Thus a chief executive officer might be punished for the same misdeed as the corporation. This proposal acknowledges the ambiguity of agency, but it has drawbacks. If we were dealing with individuals, such a duplication of culpability would be objectionable, an evasion of the main issue, who exactly *was* responsible. It also raises moral doubts, because the sense in which a corporation is responsible is irreducibly different from that in which people are.

The influence of artificial persons can be seen at work here. Paul Brietzke suggests that "sending [the] . . . executives to jail would offer a stronger deterrent than does punishing the corporation, a punishment that is usually visited on shareholders and that is easily rationalized." But as we have seen, executives tend to act in goal-defined positions, and others count on them to do so. None acts in his own name.[17] We confront the old questions: who did it, and who is responsible? But trying to revive the individual paradigm in this context seems hopeless.

I conclude that it is implausible to treat a corporation as a member of the human community, a member with a personality (but not a face), intentions (but no feelings), relationships (but no family or friends), responsibility (but no conscience), and susceptibility to punishment (but no capacity for pain).[18] In the

[16] See French, *Collective and Corporate Responsibility*, 113–14, 179–80.

[17] Paul Brietzke, "A Law and Economics of Coercion," paper presented at a symposium on "Law and the Legitimation of Violence," held at State University of New York, Buffalo, Mar. 1988, 6.

[18] French acknowledges that some moral predicates can't be applied to corporations: "Corporations cannot be bigamists or rapists, but the fact that they do

history of corporate misbehavior humans have had to pit themselves against *im*personal corporate entities and have even jeopardized their human welfare to get legal redress of harms done to them. Such problems as these the metaphysical personhood of corporations leaves unsolved.

III

Alexander Hamilton opposed having multiple agents in the executive branch of government because "it often becomes impossible, amidst mutual accusations, to determine on whom the blame or the punishment of a pernicious measure . . . ought really to fall. . . . The circumstances which may have led to any national miscarriage or misfortune are sometimes so complicated that . . . though we may clearly see upon the whole that there has been mismanagement, yet it may be impracticable to pronounce to whose account the evil which may have been incurred is truly chargeable." [19]

The composite nature of corporate action effects what Brietzke calls a "sea-change." He tells that when Ford Motor Company's executives refused to redesign the Pinto, which had been proved hazardous, choosing "to kill several people [was] something they would . . . not choose to do in their private capacities." Thus, "an organizational rationality . . . need not be the simple sum of its members' or leaders' rationalities." [20]

As we have seen, the corporate atmosphere, with its empha-

---

not have the capacities needed to commit those crimes has no general effect on their status vis-à-vis the criminal law per se. . . . The notion of criminal liability has never been framed in such way that those who may be found guilty of some crimes may be found guilty for all or any crimes in the corpus"; *Collective and Corporate Responsibility*, 174.

[19] Alexander Hamilton, John Jay, and James Madison, *The Federalist Papers* (New York: New American Library, 1961), No. 60, 428. Hamilton thought that it was better to have public focus on one executive "who, from the very circumstance of his being alone, will be more narrowly watched and more readily suspected"; 430.

[20] Brietzke, "Law and Economics of Coercion," 5–7. Brietzke adds that "the insiders can take refuge in their anonymity and, often, in their *de facto* immunity." French also makes the point that corporate motives and individual motives for corporate action can differ; *Collective and Corporate Responsibility*, 41, 47. But while Brietzke includes simple collectives like mobs among his examples, French excludes them because, lacking a CID structure, they don't formally identify responsible agents in decisions.

sis on roles, affects those making decisions and encourages them to focus on a single purpose. A framework is thus created where moral considerations are blocked from view, where people allow themselves to do what they might otherwise shrink from. David Luban distinguishes three dimensions of the situation:

Psychologically, role players in such organizations lack the emotional sense that they are morally responsible for the consequences of organizational behavior. . . . Politically, responsibility cannot be localized on the organizational chart, and thus in some real . . . way no one—no *one*—ever is responsible. Morally, role players have insufficient information to be confident that they are in a position to deliberate effectively, because bureaucratic organizations parcel out information along functional lines.[21]

Lack of information and lack of responsibility go hand in hand, and both are built into the organizational structure.

The idea of corporate personhood might still be defended in the following way. The word "person" has many applications that are morally neutral and not connected to moral judgment. Thus, as French says, a person has a personality, a location, a history, a way of looking at the world: in all these respects a corporation might qualify as a person. Since the moral import of "person" is only one aspect of its use, why can't we say that what we mean by calling a corporation a person is that it is a person without the moral import of that term? That is simply part of the fiction.

The proposal is that a person, legally speaking, doesn't have to be a moral subject, that some non-moral persons can be allowed. Can we recognize such entities as these? No, it is impossible, because other features of being a person, such as having rights and being entitled to respect and membership in the community—all of which corporations desire—are connected with human capacities and with moral responsibility.[22] A person who is not a subject for morals is an anomaly.

[21] David Luban, *Lawyers and Justice* (Princeton, N.J.: Princeton University Press, 1989), 123.

[22] Donaldson proposes that we look at corporations, not as persons, but as entities that need and want some of the rights of persons. Recognizing this, the society and its members should make certain demands of them, demands regarding treatment of workers and effects of corporate actions on the larger community. Companies that fail to uphold their side of the contract forfeit their right

IV

Let us look at the means by which corporate entities act, and turn multiple actions into a single action, for this too raises particular problems. Decisions of boards and committees are commonly made by voting, where the majority determines the action. Church councils of elders operate this way, as do most university departments, professional groups, and informal clubs; so do corporate boards and parliaments. But such decision making poses problems. Of course, majority rule is not the only way for groups to make decisions and may, in fact, not be preferred from a moral view. Yet consensus, where all must agree, though morally preferable, is often thought to be too slow and thus impractical. In any case, long-standing use in Western tradition gives authority to a majority in deciding issues in a great variety of contexts.[23]

Imagine a group reaching a decision by majority vote. Put aside for the moment who carries out instructions, and focus on who makes the decision. The group may be a highly structured corporation; it may be a political party, a club, a senate or council. Hobbes would say that all such bodies turn multiple voices into one voice. The process can be compared to a projection or mapping of many views and voices onto one, analogous to the way a photograph maps or projects three dimensions onto a two-dimensional surface. The question is how to conceive the group action in terms of the moral paradigm.

Suppose the deliberations of a corporate committee culminate in a vote showing a clear majority, say five to three, in favor of an action, which is then executed. Procedurally, the decision is unexceptionable. But suppose that the action decided on is both offensive and illegal, perhaps the prohibited dumping of pollutants into a river or the violation of federally mandated safety requirements.

Like other artificial persons the body takes action in the name of authors, here the stockholders. Yet although the action may

---

to the fictional status of persons. Such a contract has both moral and legal force; *Corporations and Morality*, 41–52.

[23] While Athenians practiced majority rule in their assembly and courts, they were well aware of its shortcomings; Aristophanes exposes some in *The Knights* and other works. I discuss the moral aspects of majority rule in *The Grammar of Justice* (Ithaca, N.Y.: Cornell University Press, 1987), chap. 3.

be taken for their (financial) advantage, the stockholders are unaware of the decision. They are insulated just as an incompetent person is insulated from what her guardian does.

Imagine then that the misdeed is discovered by the authorities, and action is taken against the corporate board. How does this work? The board may argue that its members do not decide as individuals, but as part of a composite agent with a circumscribed function to represent others. Thus they cannot be assumed to have done as individuals what the board did; each only tried to fulfill the duties of the position. To hold members individually responsible involves a category mistake, like mistaking the movements of molecules for movements of a machine they are part of.

There is an odd consequence of this attractive argument. If their role exculpates the members of the board from responsibility, the same should be true when the committee is a committee of the whole and represents no one outside itself but only its members. For the argument is exactly the same: the members would not do *as individuals* what they feel their role requires, never mind that that role is the role of representing themselves, of being their own agents.[24] And the same argument applies when decisions are made by consensus.

Return to the board's action with this additional detail: a majority votes to do something illegal, while a minority questions and argues vehemently against doing it. When charges are brought for the illegal action, how should dissenting members be treated? Both as individuals and members, they dissociated themselves from the opinion of the majority. Are they still partly responsible for the body's decision? And if so, are they equally culpable with the majority members?

Hobbes saw the problem and gave an unequivocal answer: all members are equally authors of the action, and all are equally culpable. In the political case, he insisted, citizens are equally and individually responsible for the actions of the sovereign. That they are many and divided and that the sovereign is one

---

[24]Examples are those "professional corporations" of doctors and dentists, among others. One wonders if all the represented parties being present and voting has some influence on what policies are proposed and supported. The fact that a corporate board is usually small compared to those represented and often meets in private session may affect what policies emerge.

makes no difference to their authorship.[25] But this result is counterintuitive. Why are members voting against the measure equally culpable with the others? Why are they culpable at all? At this point the example needs further development. If the minority, or some of them, were in favor of *even more objectionable* alternatives, or an objectionable alternative less likely to be discovered, then their culpability becomes plausible even though they were outvoted. This shows that, in the end, their reasons for voting are as morally significant as the votes themselves.

Now, suppose that of the three members of the minority, two voted on legal and moral grounds—because they thought the action irresponsible and illegal. They voiced these objections and defended them vigorously, but in the end they were outvoted. When the policy later runs into legal trouble, are they still in some degree responsible?

The committee is supposed to make policy under the body's bylaws, the CID. It is given this kind of responsibility. But most criminal punishments pertain uniquely to humans. The committee cannot be jailed any more than it can be humiliated. Only a metaphor connects it to humans, and its actions to human actions. For instance, a committee can't decide in the sense that a human can, nor can it reason or ponder. The cash value of these verbs lies in what individual members do, and this leads toward the conclusion that the individual members of the committee took the actions and must be held responsible, if anyone is.

Here we gravitate toward the widely rejected view that actions of a corporate body *must be* reducible to actions of individuals. But before rushing into this, let us return to the position of minority members. Suppose the dissenters did everything possible to dissuade the others from their course. A commonsense view is that then they did nothing wrong. Yet since they participated in the decision and were parties to it and without their presence the committee could not have acted (i.e., not having a quorum), they cannot be altogether dissociated from what was

[25] *Leviathan* (Hammondsworth, Engl.: Penguin, 1961), I:16, 221. Hobbes is certainly thinking here of the case where a senate may speak for the citizens. Since the senators don't decide as individual agents, they must be counted among the authors, Hobbes seems to reason. And if a minority of senators could disclaim responsibility, that would put the universal authorship of the action in jeopardy, along with the ability of the multitude to be united through having a representative. I discuss political representation in Chapter 6.

done. Suppose they resigned in protest immediately after the vote. Would that exonerate them? Intuitively one wants to say yes, but corporate agency poses the familiar obstacles: the committee is nothing without its members, they help constitute it. Therefore its action cannot be dissociated from them even if it also cannot be reduced to actions of theirs.

Perhaps resigning *before* the vote would have done the trick, for the action would then be taken without their participation. But they might then merit criticism for not having tried their best to prevent the decision, for not trying to change the opinions of the others up to the end. Furthermore, they may have been unable to foresee how the vote would go. How then would they conscientiously refuse to exert their influence?

If minority members are held responsible for decisions they oppose, then they face a troubling dilemma: either they are culpable for the action they participated in, or, if they decline to participate, they are censurable for not attempting to influence a decision they thought wrong. The dilemma is real.

On the other side is a dilemma too. If the minority members aren't held responsible, then it is strange to say that *the committee* was the agent, for the five members who voted for the policy, while a majority, are not what is meant by "the committee." They cannot speak or act as a committee without including the others. So even though practically they determine the action, it can't be attributed to them. One might say that they are morally responsible for what they did *as individuals*, for their affirmative votes. But it is not their votes that violated the law.

v

Virginia Held and Emile Durkheim would say that the responsibility of each member is to the role. They aren't acting as themselves but as someone else, as Hobbes would put it. And Milton Friedman would argue that managing a shareholder's money entails fiduciary responsibilities, those of a financial shepherd, which insulate managers from their responsibilities to the larger society.[26] We have met this problem before: limiting responsibil-

[26] See Friedman, "The Social Responsibility of Business Is to Increase Its Profits," *New York Times Magazine*, Sept. 13, 1970.

ity to *role* duties makes an agent's life too simple for serious moral evaluation. It makes a two-dimensional projection of the multidimensional, morally charged substance of a human life. This doesn't mean that the job of managing shareholders' investments imposes no moral responsibility: it does, and so do other jobs. The question is whether this responsibility operates to the exclusion of other kinds.

There is another source of confusion in the structure of corporations. While managers and boards are protected by their positions, investors are also protected by the corporation's design. It is commonly said that one advantage of incorporation is "that the liability of investors in a company may be limited . . . [since they have] the assurance that, if mistakes are made . . . they will not be called upon to pay the creditors out of their own pockets."[27] But if they own the company and the company owes debts, why aren't stockholders liable for them, as Hobbes would insist they are? If they aren't, then clearly nobody is, which means that the corporation serves the recognized purpose of exculpating investors from both financial and moral responsibility for what is done in their name. Its design screens them from accountability.

With the structure of corporations go the problems of attitude toward accountability that we have already encountered. The judge who presided in the *Dalkon Shield* case describes what he found:

> The project manager for Dalkon Shield explains that a particular question should have gone to the medical department, the medical representative explains that the question was really in the bailiwick of the quality control department, and the quality control department representative explains that the project manager was the one with the authority to make a decision on that question. . . . It is not at all unusual for the hard questions . . . to be unanswerable by anyone from Robins.[28]

---

[27] Clark, *The Japanese Company*, 2. French, on the other hand, sees no reason why stockholders should not be held responsible for corporate misdeeds since they undertook a risk and "in many cases the stockholder stands to benefit from the undetected crime"; *Collective and Corporate Responsibility*, 188. It is a curious kind of responsibility, however, that is thus disengaged both from intentions and from knowledge of what was being done.

[28] In re A. H. Robins Co., Inc., "Dalkon Shield" IUD Product Liability Litigation, 575 F. Supp. 718 (Dist. of Kansas, 1978), at 724; quoted by Luban, *Lawyers and Justice*, 124.

The value of corporations is as obvious to both American officers and investors as the practice of *ringi* is to the Japanese.

V I

To deal socially with corporate persons without the fiction of personhood, Thomas Donaldson proposes that there is a contractual relation between businesses and the community that creates responsibilities for them.[29] He says of large corporations,

they affect the lives of millions of people, influence foreign policy, and employ [many] . . . people. . . . Equally important is the fact that General Motors exists only through the cooperation and commitment of society. It draws its employees from society, sells its goods to society, and is given its status by society. . . . If General Motors holds society responsible for providing the conditions of its existence, then for what does society hold General Motors responsible?

A number of things. Donaldson requires at minimum "that *productive organizations avoid deception or fraud, that they show respect for their workers as human beings, and that they avoid any practice that systematically worsens the situation of a given group in society.*"[30] Corporations on his account can be required to be involved in community matters and to participate in its projects. That would transform their status as convenient artificial persons and give them a distinctive place in society, give them a quasi-moral status of their own.

The idea faces familiar opponents, however. Theodore Leavitt says bluntly that "welfare and society are not the corporation's business. Its business is making money. . . . Government's job is not business, and business's job is not government. And unless these functions are resolutely separated in all respects, they are eventually combined in every respect." By this argument, then, business has its function, to make money, while government's function concerns social welfare; better to not mix the two. Moreover, "the results of single-minded devotion to profit should be invigorating. With none of the corrosive distractions and costly bureaucracies that now serve the pious cause of wel-

---

[29] Rita Manning also argues for corporate responsibilities without the fiction of personhood; "Corporate Responsibility and Corporate Personhood," *Journal of Business Ethics* 3 (1984): 77–84.

[30] Donaldson, *Corporations and Morality*, 42, 53; italics in original.

fare . . . management can shoot for the economic moon," he argues. "Altruism, self-denial, charity . . . are vital in certain walks of our life. . . . But for the most part those virtues are alien to competitive economics."[31]

Corporations aren't the only entities with productive economic functions, but they are the most numerous and powerful and the kind most intimately connected with a free enterprise economy. Economist Robert Heilbroner, quoting John Kenneth Galbraith, observes that it is only the "mythology of capitalism" that "power is wielded most effectively and efficiently by the single entrepreneur." On the contrary, "it is the committee system with its combination of impersonality, specialization, and bureaucratic procedure, that has proven indispensable."[32] These characteristics of committees are precisely the ones that give artificial persons their moral advantage, by creating amoral contexts where actions are not done by anyone. Thus one speculates that the "efficiency" Heilbroner and Galbraith attribute to committees and bureaucracies relates to their operating, as other artificial persons do, in a moral limbo.

In sum, treating corporations like persons is morally hazardous. For the fiction of a person without any moral dimension is a modern Gyges ring, an invitation to act without accountability.

[31] Leavitt, "Dangers of Social Responsibility," 139, 141–42.
[32] Richard Heilbroner, *Between Capitalism and Socialism* (New York: Random House, 1970), 230.

SIX

The State as Servant

What, then, is the government? . . . A body charged with the execution of the laws and the maintenance of freedom.

Jean-Jacques Rousseau, *The Social Contract*

WE TURN NOW to problems with understanding government as an artificial person. The idea that a state arises from an agreement between individuals accounts for political authority and justifies it. Thanks to that contract, a government can speak for the citizens, and they are responsible for whatever it does. It seems obvious that a state is useful, because it allows a people to do things they could not do otherwise, such as incur a foreign debt.[1] And it is difficult to see how some kind of agent can be dispensed with here, as Hobbes says. At the same time, however, the idea that citizens are responsible for whatever their government does is profoundly troublesome.

Sovereignty is the form of government Hobbes preferred, but his concept embraced other forms, including a parliamentary one. Yet when representative government is substituted for an absolutist one, representation becomes immensely complicated, as in a modern government where there are many kinds of representative—legislative, judicial, and executive—all speaking and acting for citizens simultaneously. But they have in common that the idea of artificial person underlies them all, and I argue that the problems that characterize other forms of artificial persons recur here and go to the heart of what political representation means.

An important difference between a theory of sovereignty and

---

[1] In American history, incurring a national debt was given as a reason for having a central government with the general power to tax.

most theories of representative government is the way each kind pictures the citizens. Hobbes's citizens are not expected to judge beyond their private interests, many of them short-sighted; but by means of reason they come to include among their interests the value of having a government. The details of ruling can be left to someone else, though; they hold no intrinsic interest for the citizen.[2]

A democratic system, however, posits citizens of a different kind, who stand in a different relation to their public officials and are expected to involve themselves in government. They advise and continually subject government decisions to criticism, and they show their unhappiness at the polling place. Thus Hobbes's theory has to be rethought for representative government. And the question needs to be raised, as it could not be raised in Hobbes: what is the responsibility of representative government to citizens?

I

The contract that people presumably make with one another, that puts them all under a common authority, serves to unite them: they become one agent in speech and action. Unity is government's first function. Yet when it comes to responsibility for government's actions, the multitude remain many. Citizens are directly responsible for what the government does: its debts become their individual debts, its promises theirs to keep, and its offenses are ascribable to them.[3] This is what it means to have government act in one's name. Hobbes would say, this is what it means to have a government.

But can responsibility be made so easily to devolve on the citizens? How can they be held individually responsible for everything a government does? They cannot be culpable for its ac-

---

[2] I explore the peculiar marriage of Hobbes's social atomism and democratic thought in chapter 3 of *The Grammar of Justice* (Ithaca, N.Y.: Cornell University Press, 1987). Combining these two sets of assumptions is no doubt responsible for some knotty theoretical problems concerning political representation.

[3] The implications of this kind of representation were a profound concern of the colonial framers of the Constitution. While Hamilton argued for a broad federal power of taxation, his opponents objected to the idea that whatever the government chose to spend the citizens must pay for, since the latter lacked control. The framework of both arguments is Hobbesian.

tions any more than other authors can for their representatives. Hobbes's answer is that there is no other kind of action for citizens than action through representatives of some kind, that the artificial person of the state gives all meaning there is to the political action. There is no other locus for responsibility, and citizens have no platform from which to criticize.

Yet in the contemporary picture of participatory government, moral accountability is often demanded. Elected figures are required to explain and justify their votes and to dismiss appointees who misbehave. The elected representative depends upon election and can be discharged for misbehavior or violation of his representative trust.[4] This gives a new twist to the concept of sovereign government. Instead of a Leviathan with arbitrary power to coerce, government now is a servant, beholden to its citizen masters. With this understanding of representation, Hobbes's free-wheeling giant seems to have been domesticated and tamed, the imperious ruler transformed into a muscular and useful inferior. Therefore the inference is at hand that, in contrast to the sovereign state, representative government can be held up to the light of morality and will meet its test. Ordinary moral considerations can be introduced into the realm of political representation. That, at least, is how it appears.

There would seem to be a great theoretical advantage in a servant government, primarily because it reconciles a legitimate, central authority with Rousseau's idea that sovereignty resides in and cannot leave the people.[5] Representative government is *of* the people; that means the citizen-masters are in control, broadly speaking, and representatives are accountable to the constituents. There seems to be a clear line by which moral responsibility can be traced.

II

Conceiving government as an artificial person yields the following picture. Government action, either external or domestic, is

[4] I will deal chiefly with elected representatives, since they raise problems not raised before. The moral position of appointed figures is similar in many respects to that of nonpolitical forms of artificial person.

[5] For Rousseau the citizens must originally be capable of political action and, unlike idiots, must be competent as political authors. This conception raises the question whether citizens must have a government in order to take political action. Hobbes says that they must, for they need the unity an artificial person

necessarily done at a personal distance. The citizenry, who are the authors represented, retain full responsibility, while the political actor or agent impersonates them in political matters. But here, as with other artificial persons, the author is missing an essential part of autonomous action and cannot have responsibility in the paradigmatic sense. The problem is enhanced in a complex democratic system, Dennis Thompson argues, where many hands are involved in actions. "When citizens look for officials to call to account for a policy, they rarely find anyone who single-handedly made the policy."[6]

Nonetheless representation by a servant government suggests a way for citizens to monitor and judge political actions, since as masters they retain general control through elections. If someone acts in our name, we can require that she act honorably; in this respect accountability appears palpable. Yet the underlying moral problem is that the electorate is *not* fully responsible for the misdeeds of their representatives; they did not make her choices. And acting in someone else's name, the representative cannot take full responsibility as she would for private decisions. Then is the idea of the servant government representing and accountable to the electorate an unrealistic vision?

I propose that there are indeed serious problems with such a theory, chiefly those associated with artificial persons. First, it fails—as do other kinds of artificial persons—to come to terms with the moral vocabulary. It is not simply that the buck stops with more than one individual, or with the wrong one, but that it doesn't stop. A second problem is the way this conception affects representatives and public servants morally—how, as with other artificial persons, it influences their view of themselves and shapes their character. This consequence has to be factored into the justification of the theory.

III

Hanna Pitkin acknowledges a tension in a representative's position: he is obligated on the one hand "to do what is best for

---

gives them. But getting together for their original contract, they constituted a unity of sorts. The making of the contract thus poses difficult questions for Hobbes.

[6]Dennis Thompson, *Political Ethics and Public Office* (Cambridge, Mass.: Harvard University Press, 1987), 40.

those he represents"; but on the other hand he has an obligation "to be responsive to [their] wishes. He need not always obey them, but he must consider them." Is occasional conflict between him and his constituents inevitable then? Not necessarily, says Pitkin, for he has a further obligation "to act in such a way that, although he is independent . . . no conflict arises between them."[7] His mission is double: both to "do what is best" for voters, and to make them content with what he does. These conditions set the stage for political manipulation and deception and for the problem of "dirty hands." The problem is described by Michael Walzer: a political action "may be exactly the right thing to do . . . and yet leave the man who does it guilty of a moral wrong." The necessity to act in such a way is, in Walzer's view and that of many others, an inescapable feature of public life.[8] Moreover one would not want a representative who was a moral "absolutist" or "innocent," who refused to soil his hands for the greater social good.[9]

In Sarte's play titled *Dirty Hands*, Hugo, a young idealist, protests against the party leader's willingness to cooperate with the party's political enemies: "For years you will have to cheat, trick, and maneuver. . . . You'll have to defend the reactionary measures taken by the government in which you participate." Hoerderer answers: "But we have always told lies. . . . I'll lie when I must. . . . All means are good when they're effective"—provided that the end is justified. Hoerderer scorns moral scruple in politics: "Purity is an idea of a yogi or a monk," unworkable

[7] Hanna Pitkin, *The Concept of Representation* (Berkeley: University of California Press, 1967), 164, 162, 166.

[8] Michael Walzer, "Political Action: The Problem of Dirty Hands," *Philosophy and Public Affairs* 2, 1 (Fall 1972): 161. I omit Walzer's qualification, "in utilitarian terms," since it does not affect my argument. However, many writers who share his view about dirty hands are, like him, utilitarians.

[9] The first adjective is Walzer's; the second Peter Johnson's in *Politics, Innocence and the Limits of Goodness* (New York: Routledge, Chapman and Hall, 1989). However, Walzer insists that we would not want an official who failed to feel guilt, "to be ruled by men who have lost their souls," but this only deepens the moral dilemma, he realizes; "Political Action," 177. Bernard Williams proposes that we need to modify our demands "from both ends, allowing both that the good need not be as pure as all that, so long as they retain some active sense of moral costs and moral limits; and that the society has some genuinely settled politics and some expectations of civic responsibility"; "Politics and Moral Character," in S. Hampshire, ed., *Public and Private Morality* (Cambridge, Eng.: Cambridge University Press, 1978), 69.

in the real political world. Peter Johnson adds that "moral inno-cence is a proper disqualification from politics. . . . It makes pol-itics impossible."[10]

My discussion of dirty hands differs from these in two re-spects. For one thing, I am interested not only in the actions required of an individual by institutions, but in the institutions that demand them.[11] I consider problematic actions in context, where the context itself is subject to criticism, where the goals of politics and the shape of the political institutions are presumed to be given and inflexible. In this framework the "paradox" of the relation between virtue and politics that Johnson stresses disappears. On the contrary, institutional contexts are no more exempt from moral criticism than are other human actions.

Also, I do not connect moral responsibility with purity and innocence, with their implications of inexperience. The uncanny innocence of Melville's Billy Budd and the purity of saints are not crucial in locating moral responsibility.[12] On the contrary, I argue, human experience, with its fumbling and mistakes, re-grets and corrections, is essential to mature moral judgment and moral understanding. A person's political actions need to be seen as part of this whole, as what W. Kenneth Howard calls "an extended dimension of our own lives" where "the moral uni-verse is not deserted but expanded."[13] For this extension, moral

[10] Jean-Paul Sartre, *No Exit and Three Other Plays*, 221, 223–24; Johnson, *Politics*, 248. Against such reasoning, R. F. Holland argues that it is not purity but politics that is "impossible," because politics involves compromise. In it "you have to compromise with evil" and do evil. He and Thomas Nagel would agree that the root of the problem is consequentialist ethics. For that is "an ethic that sanctions the doing of evil: it lets in propositions like 'This is an evil thing to do but I am justified' and 'It is evil but I must do it'." And evil is what one *should not* do; that is exactly why Holland rejects consequentialism and, with it, politics; "Absolute Ethics, Mathematics and the Impossibility of Politics," in Holland, *Against Empir-icism* (Totowa, N.J.: Barnes & Noble, 1980), 136.

[11] Walzer and Johnson draw heavily upon dilemmas portrayed in fiction, es-pecially by existentialists like Sartre and Camus, which frame the problem in terms of a lonely individual who must act, sometimes tragically. This simplifies the issue and turns attention away from the individual-in-context I am concerned with, where many kinds of moral relations are relevant—institutional ones as well as a variety of others.

[12] It is arguable that purity and innocence fall altogether outside the province of morality, that both preclude the struggling of humans with their conflicting aims, their imperfection, and their capacity for guilt and remorse.

[13] W. Kenneth Howard, "Must Public Hands Be Dirty?" *The Journal of Value Inquiry* 11, 1 (Spring 1977); 38–39.

purity and unmarred innocence are beside the point, and decision making may be hard without departing from the context of morality.

I V

Unlike Walzer and Johnson, Thomas Nagel connects the dirty-hands issue with the justifiability of institutions that require them. "The degree to which ruthlessness is acceptable in public life—the ways in which public actors may have to get their hands dirty—depends on moral features of the institutions through which public action is carried out." Nevertheless, in the public sphere "impersonal aspects are more prominent than in any assessment of individual actions," and they should be. Public officials "accept special obligations to serve interests that their offices are designed to advance. . . . In doing so, they correlatively reduce their right to consider other factors, both their personal interests and more general ones not related to the institution or their role in it." They lose not only their obligation but their right to be guided by usual moral standards: public service "warrants methods usually excluded for private individuals, and sometimes it licenses ruthlessness . . . [which] can be explained only by a direct application of moral theory to those public institutions that create the roles to which public obligations are tied." [14] The justification of otherwise questionable actions lies in the justification of the institution that requires it.

There is another moral hazard in giving priority to public obligations, for public offices "have a profound effect on the behavior of the individuals who fill them, an effect partly restrictive but significantly liberating. . . . They can produce a feeling of moral insulation that has strong attractions." The duties which both bind and free a representative and "the sense that one is the agent of vast impersonal forces or the servant of institutions larger than an individual—all these ideas form a heady and sometimes corrupting brew." Thus public office "nourishes the illusion that personal morality does not apply to it with any force." [15]

[14] Thomas Nagel, "Ruthlessness in Public Life," in *Mortal Questions* (Cambridge, Eng.: Cambridge University Press, 1979), 89, 82.

[15] Ibid., 76, 77. Johnson describes the problem similarly: "Public activity involves the obligations of office which are not reducible to individual duties. It is

Since political duties are defined in terms of larger institutions, immoral behavior can only be justified by justifying the need for the institutions and their need for such behavior. If a given institution is justified and its requirements are necessary to its functioning, then and only then is the requirement of morally troubling behavior permissible. This way of justifying shady action is analogous to the "adversary system excuse" for lawyers; both say that if the system's goals and general function are justified, that can justify immoral behavior of individuals. John Rawls takes a similar line with respect to political office: "if the basic structure of society is just, or as just as it is reasonable to expect in the circumstances, everyone has a natural duty to do what is required of him" by his position in the structure.[16] The shadow of role morality is traced here clearly.

The justification is not as simple as it may sound, however. For one thing, Nagel conceives that the justification of an institution should take into account the viewpoint and interests of every individual through some kind of representative system. For another, he requires that an official should object to role demands that do not conform to the broad mission of government, for that mission has precedence over all other institutional obligations.[17] He must evaluate his official responsibilities in this broader framework. Let us look more closely at all these features.

v

Nagel justifies institutions from only one side, the side of benefits to the society as a whole. If that benefit is large enough, it

possible that such obligations can only be fulfilled by conduct which would otherwise be regarded as morally blameworthy"; *Politics*, 247. A parallel point relates to military duties: Anthony Hartle says that "the military professional, in the preparation for and conduct of war, takes actions which would not be permissible outside that role." That role and the military itself are justified by the values of the society, which they defend and which supports them; *Moral Issues in Military Decision Making* (Lawrence: University Press of Kansas, 1989), 32.

[16] John Rawls, *A Theory of Justice* (Cambridge, Mass.: Harvard University Press, 1971), 334. However, unlike Nagel, Rawls does not measure the justice of an institution by utilitarian considerations. Rawls's position is that "from the standpoint of the theory of justice, the most important natural duty is that to support and to further just institutions"; ibid.

[17] Nagel, "Ruthlessness," 84, 80–81. Representatives may be majoritarian and utilitarian, Nagel says, or they may consider each individual's viewpoint separately. He prefers the latter.

justifies dirty hands. But one can evaluate an institution from a very different side, that of its effects on people working in and around it. This aspect is often neglected in modern discussions, thanks to the seventeenth- and eighteenth-century social atomists who put stress on individual interests. But in both Plato and Aristotle, one important duty assigned to government was care for the moral well-being of the citizens, for improving them as citizens and for not doing them harm—particularly moral harm. Indeed the only harm that could be done one was to one's soul, one's character, Socrates argued. So if, as Nagel says, the obligations of a public servant form "a heady and sometimes corrupting brew," which demands the loosening of one's commitment to morality, that might raise a serious question in one's mind about the position's justification. Notice that arguing from the moral effects on individuals is just as consequentialist as Nagel's or Walzer's reasoning; but instead of looking at the public and outward consequences of political actions, it gazes back on those who participate in them and the moral impact it has on these creatures who are acknowledged to be susceptible to corruption. It provides a general argument against dirty hands. For as the political artificial person acts, not only for our benefit, but in our name, we have powerful reason for feeling uneasy about putting him in a position that damages his character. It is worse morally than subjecting him to physical danger, as happens with military personnel.

Among the goods that benefit a society and give reason for its institutional arrangements must be counted the good character of the citizens. An account of the effects of an institution on the characters of those in it belongs somewhere in the moral picture. If we see institutions merely as the principal political agents, then individuals become the passive recipients of benefits. But there is another way to view them. As Kenneth Howard argues, government is also a context in which individuals act, where some of their lives are carried out, and their characters are shaped for better or worse.

This moral impact of institutions on participants can be seen at closer range in Nagel's demand that a representative be able to evaluate and sometimes constrain what his position requires, not take its justification for granted. An official should not engage in *unjustified* "dirty-hands" behavior.[18] But separating the justified demands of public service from unjustified ones requires a keen faculty of moral criticism, and that faculty is just what continued participation in an institution brings into jeopardy. Such jobs, Nagel says, may corrupt or at least soften the holder's capacity for moral objection. Once accustomed to ignoring moral constraints, does an individual retain her ability to judge and evaluate? Being inured to morally objectionable requirements, how firm is her purchase on moral criticism?

Overall Nagel approves of putting large decisions in the hands of representatives. This constitutes a "moral division of labor between society and the individual," which he finds generally beneficial. It liberates the represented, leaving us "free to lead our individual lives in obedience to more personal attachments, commitments, and crotchets."[19] But in separating the people, who are the authors, from actions done in their names, the freedom gained amounts to freedom from an active critical role, freedom from responsibility for what is done in one's name. It is freedom that an autonomous person in a democratic setting has no reason to accept.

VI

Let us look again at the position of an elected representative and her relation to constituents. Elected positions allow great latitude for choice of issues and means and for the interpretation of the role itself, as Nagel says. A senator may decide many of her own responsibilities. She doesn't need an impersonal demeanor or to be part of the background against which others act; she is at center stage. She may need to show her constituents that she resembles them, is a flesh-and-blood person who shares their concerns and is capable of acting for them. Thus she brings her full personality to the position and presents herself as someone worthy of trust. This image contrasts sharply with Nagel's representative, whose constituents are happy to be relieved of pol-

---

[18] This provision is important since it would preclude from justified "dirty-hands" behavior such misdeeds as those committed in the Iran-Contra dealings of the mid-1980's.

[19] Nagel, "Moral Conflict and Political Legitimacy," *Philosophy and Public Affairs* 13, 3 (Summer 1984): 237, 238.

icy details; and it contrasts with the image of a representative who does dirty work for our benefit. It reintroduces the relevance of moral commitment and the importance of character.

"Dirty-hands" behavior is much harder to justify in *this* picture than in one where action works impersonally toward specific ends. Here there is an ongoing debate about what policies are preferable and what means are acceptable; and the representative needs to share her information to help the constituents make their judgments. She needs to present and explore issues with them, and for such dialogue her constituents must trust her honesty. Her known tendency to deceive or withhold information or to treat people unscrupulously undermines the relationship.[20]

Without the bonds of honesty and trust that bind a representative to her constituents, democratic participation may be thwarted by cynicism. Citizens don't trust the information they are given, they doubt that they are respected; then how, they reason, can their judgments matter? Compromising honesty in return for institutional goods, Walzer says, is necessary; but if so, it puts informed citizen participation—and therefore the whole system—in jeopardy.

Walzer, Nagel, and the fictional Hoerderer of Sartre's play are concerned about goals that are important for the community. What can we say about the ones that require dirty hands to accomplish if dirty hands are disallowed? Perhaps they are reachable by other means. Or perhaps they are unattainable by any appropriate means. Then they may need to be given up; not every morally desirable goal is attainable in a morally tolerable way.

I propose that dirty-hands behavior is much more difficult to justify in a representative system than is often supposed. Relations of trust are a necessity of democratic life, not an optional good that can be traded off, even for large future benefits. Our political representatives will speak to us, as well as represent us, on morally charged matters, and we need to trust them. It is a

[20] Dennis Thompson makes the same point, arguing it is paradoxical to propose that politicians can secretly follow principles citizens don't endorse. He argues that in a democratic society the consequentialist "would have to persuade citizens of the rightness of [his moral view] through the democratic process . . . which presupposes publicity"; *Political Ethics*, 17.

two-way relationship of dialogue and action, and it is an educational process on both sides. Howard describes the task before the theorist here: we need to "examine what a theory of political morality must be in order both to coexist with our traditional ethics and get the job of public living done."[21]

I sketched in Chapter 3 a picture where a person acts autonomously, though sometimes in a very complicated context, where her decisions reflect her many relations to others. In such action responsibility for decisions remains individual; role moralities and rules cannot determine morally charged decisions, though they are often relevant. Seen from the outside, it may be difficult to analyze and to assess such decisions; one may need a good deal of detailed information. But presumably, given that information, a serious person could make that judgment. In my picture, it is impossible to say, as Dennis Thompson does, that "the sincerity of representatives or even their motives" are not the issue.[22] They are, in fact, at the heart of it. One need not suppose that difficult choices can be redescribed as clear and unequivocal ones, with a simple justification, that political decisions must be clear and easy in order to satisfy the demand of moral responsibility—that if they are not, morality must be put aside. A difficult decision requires moral wisdom, not an institutional excuse. The task is, as Howard says, to design institutions that will reflect this moral picture.

VII

In important respects Hobbes's concept is out of keeping with democracy. Hanna Pitkin protests, "Nothing could be farther from what we ordinarily think of as representation or representative government! We read the *Leviathan* and feel that somehow we have been tricked." True political representation must involve us more intimately with government and in a meaningful way: "Behind Hobbes's logical formulae lies the practical difference between being ruled by one's own representative(s) and

---

[21] Howard, "Must Public Hands Be Dirty?" 38.

[22] Thompson, *Political Ethics*, 112. He continues: "Both [sincerity and motives] are difficult enough to appraise in personal interactions. In the distant and mediated relations of political life, they can hardly be the basis for reliable judgments of legislative ethics."

being ruled by some other authority." The crux of the difference, Pitkin says, is that "representation implies standards for, or limits on, the conduct of the representative. . . . We are . . . interested in the nature of the activity itself, what goes on during representing, the substance or content of acting for others . . . some kind of activity or way of acting." We are interested in *how* our representative represents us; it is "a fiduciary relationship, involving trust and obligation on both sides."[23]

Unlike the lawyer who is hired to serve some purpose, where he uses his discretion about the means, a political representative's job is not focused only on beneficial ends. His relation to constituents is important and must be continually developed and reappraised, by him and his constituents alike. This relationship makes demands that may conflict with his other moral responsibilities, true, but its moral coloring is beyond challenge.

A different conception is advanced by Edmund Burke; he held that while the people choose their representative, they cannot presume to guide his policy choices and need not be expected to agree with them. Still, the representative speaks and acts for them, as well as for the larger community. In that process he makes decisions that they can't be expected to understand. "The most poor, illiterate, and uninformed creatures upon earth . . . ought never to be called into council about [the cause or the right remedy of problems]. . . . They ought to be totally shut out; because their reason is weak; . . . because, they want [that is, lack] information." It would be a mistake for representatives to take instruction from their uninformed constituents, to be influenced by them, or try to instruct them. More explicitly than Hobbes, Burke conceives government like the guardian of an idiot or a baby; the people are incapable of deciding intelligently for themselves. Thus, a representative judges, and should judge, in the people's name and for their good; that is what responsible government means. "The king is the representative of the people; so are the lords; so are the judges. They all are trustees for the people . . . because no power is given for the sole sake of the holder."[24] Government is there to save people from themselves, to serve their interests whether they understand

[23] Pitkin, *Concept of Representation*, 34, 36, 32, 114, 128.
[24] Edmund Burke, *Reflections on the Revolution in France and Other Works*, in Hanna Pitkin, ed., *Representation* (New York: Atherton, 1969), 172, 164.

them or not. Therefore every difference between the representative's and the constituents' beliefs is tolerable.[25]

In giving authority about what constitutes community welfare to the representative, Burke may seem to solve the problem of fragmented action and dissipated responsibility. For he implies that the representative is unequivocally responsible for what she does; her political deeds are first and last hers, though she does them for the benefit of others; the people have no role except in choosing who should act in their name. This view helps illuminate the dynamic of the problems of representation. Even though the representative acts entirely from her own judgment, she does not exercise that judgment *as an individual* but as the agent of other interests. And she acts not only for the interests of her constituents, but for the whole nation. Thus her decisions cannot be seen as those of a private individual or be judged in ordinary moral terms. They are made in an impersonal framework that contains competing ideas of people's good, one where justifications like Nagel's come into play. If representing the best interests of the constituents requires duplicity and chicanery, then it does.

The Burkean idea gives an emphasis to integrity, but not to honest communication with citizens. The representative who wants to be reelected needs to cultivate some of the trust that is at the heart of participatory government but not trust in his candid communication with them. His constituents need to accept their inability to criticize, and, given his custodial position, he can easily justify deceiving them, just the way a guardian might deceive an idiot in his charge.

In one sense, the Burkean representative has fuller scope for expressing her moral character, since she isn't accountable for all her deliberations about policy. She acts autonomously, it seems. At the same time, her character is the more exposed, since she lacks the excuse that she is only doing her job in carrying out the people's will. Finally, when she runs for reelection, she must answer in some coin or other to her constituents, but Burke does not tell us how this can be managed.

[25] Bentham made fun of Burke's "virtual representation" and its compatibility with autocracy: " 'Happily for you,' said Muley Ishmael once to the people of Morocco . . . 'you are bound by no laws but what have your virtual consent; for they are all made by your virtual representative, and I am he' "; *Works of Jeremy Bentham*, ed. John Bowring (Simpkin, Marshall & Co., 1843), vol. 5, 235.

VIII

Like other artificial arrangements, political representation tends to create a region of amorality where a representative acts, but not as an individual, and in this region reasons of political expediency are given currency. The institution works to frustrate the conditions of moral responsibility and to put conflicting demands on a representative. On the one hand, he should show integrity in his actions; on the other, he should observe the wishes of his constituents. It is the artificial person that causes difficulty and resolves it by legitimizing dirty hands.

To make this clearer, compare acting through a representative to a system where policy decisions are made by the citizens directly, without an intermediary. There, one presumes, responsibility does not become diffused, and the citizens are collectively responsible for what they do. It is they who act foolishly or irresponsibly, in good faith or with deceit. They act in their own names and collectively, in their collective name. They are like a defendant pleading his own case. It is only when an intermediary—a government or representative—intervenes that the familiar problems arise, and ambiguities are introduced that defy clarification.

In ancient Athens, political representation was often realized in a different and interesting way, namely, through the rotation of political and judicial offices chosen by lot. For instance, the ten tribes of Athens each chose their representatives (*prytanes*) by lot and sent them to participate in the government at Athens. These councils sent by each of the tribes then presided for one tenth of the year apiece, the order of their presiding again determined by lot. When its turn came to govern, each council chose its leader by lot. In their judicial system, as in ours, jurors were chosen by lot and thus, as one author says, "an opportunity was given to every citizen at some time to share in the administration of justice."[26] These representatives-by-lot were not chosen to represent some particular views, any more than a modern ju-

---

[26] William Morey, *Outlines of Greek History* (New York: American Book Company, 1908), 221–22. The system was not like ours with respect to the list jurors were chosen from, however, since Greek jurors were drawn from a list of volunteers for jury service. Nancy Schwartz describes a somewhat different system of rotation in Renaissance Florence; *The Blue Guitar* (Chicago: University of Chicago Press, 1988), 107–22.

ror is expected to represent the views of his class or district. It is understood that each judges for himself, by his own lights and standards. Eventually others will have their turn. Such a system defuses the artificial person problem and preserves personal responsibility.

Rousseau claimed that democratic politics absolutely requires the direct participation of citizens: "As soon as public service ceases to be the main concern of the citizens and they come to prefer to serve the state with their purse rather than their person, the state is already close to ruin. Are troops needed to march to war? They pay mercenaries and stay at home. Is it time to go to an assembly? They pay deputies and stay at home." Paid political service he saw as anathema to representation and to participatory government as well. Predictably, Rousseau applauded the Greek legislative assembly and the Athenians' continual, active exchange of opinion: "Among the Greeks, all that the people had to do, it did itself; it was continuously assembled in the market place." Representation, by contrast, is a form of corruption: "The moment a people adopts representatives it is no longer free."[27]

I X

Representative government is often viewed as morally sensitive, a form that makes both constituents and representatives responsible for their actions, one that gives government a moral dimension that sovereignty lacks. If true, this would mark an important step forward from Hobbes. Among others Jeremy Bentham thought that government could work this way, as an instrument or conduit for executing moral choices, choices that are morally

[27]Rousseau, *The Social Contract*, trans. Maurice Cranston (Middlesex, Eng.: Penguin, 1968), 140, 142–43. It does not follow that the Athenian assembly usually acted fairly or even consistently. "The citizens voted in haste and then at once proceeded to ignore what they enacted," writes J. Walter Jones in *The Law and Legal Theory of the Greeks* (London: Oxford University Press, 1956), 110. And Thucydides tells how the assembly, on the persuasions of Cleon, sent a punitive expedition to slaughter the males of Lesbos and take the women and children as slaves, in retaliation for the island's refusal to pay its yearly tribute. A ship was sent with these orders. But the next day another assembly was called, and after the tempering arguments of Diodotus, it reversed the decision and sent a ship to overtake the first and countermand the order. With heroic rowers, the second ship arrived as the edict was being read and thus prevented the brutality.

the same whether government or an individual does them. Representative government is thus better than other forms in giving full expression to the moral views of citizens and being responsible to them for what it does.

This optimistic effort to assimilate government actions to a moral model is wrong, however. My argument shows that government and its agents, insofar as they are artificial persons, are incapable of assuming moral responsibility in the sense that attaches to individuals. On the other side, democracy demands that a representative act and speak with personal integrity and relate to constituents as a responsible and three-dimensional individual. But these demands are impossible to satisfy at once.

Further, moral representation itself is inherently problematic. Moral predicates belong to individual people, not to roles or abstractions. Thus, government is an imperfect means of acting morally, even when it is used to do things that are well justified and commendable, considered as human actions. The metaphor of the state as a giant person thus misleadingly encourages us to treat state actions as surrogates for human ones. But the features of artificial persons, both single representatives and the state as a whole, block the attribution of moral responsibility. Neither as master nor as servant is the state accessible to moral predicates.

We should cease trying to see the actions of governments in human—and moral—terms and see them instead as actions of a particular kind, as governmental actions *sui generis*. That would mean an entirely different account of political representation, and it is a problem that democratic theory needs to wrestle with. One kind of shift in the meaning of representation is suggested by Joseph Tussman in an early essay. He writes:

The essence of representation is the delegation or granting of authority. . . . Within the limits of the grant of authority one is, in fact, committing himself in advance to the decision or will of another. . . . The fact that our rulers are elected does not make them any less our rulers. . . . To say that we send our representatives to Congress is not to say that we have sent our servants to the market. We have simply designated the person or persons to whose judgment or will we have subordinated ourselves. . . . An act of subordination has occurred.[28]

[28]Joseph Tussman, "The Political Theory of Thomas Hobbes," (Ph.D. diss., University of California, Berkeley, 1947), 117–18.

The government is a particular kind of entity, and its job is to govern, not to serve us. If we elect it, fine; but whether or not we do does not affect its function, which is *to rule us*. The theory of political representation ought therefore to conform itself to this reality and not try to characterize an impossible relationship of accountability. Tussman does not pretend or ask that government or political representatives be morally responsible, since that would be like making the captain accountable to the seamen or the shepherd accountable to the sheep. It would be incomprehensible in his conception.

Tussman's view is that actions of government cannot be interpreted as the actions of citizens. Whichever way we turn the servant-master relation—supposing that government owes obedience to citizens or supposing that citizens owe obedience to government—we fail to solve the issue of responsibility. Using moral standards to choose a representative is unavoidable. Moreover it is important to responsible citizenship: would we (knowingly) elect a proficient con man? Then there is the fact that we want to know what is going on; we don't accept Burke's limited idea of a citizen's capacities, but presume to judge whether our representative is acting appropriately. Our demand for moral scruple in such people is as important as our demand for openness to questions and willingness to answer.

In sum the traditional view of government as servant misleads us into thinking that political representatives are morally accountable to us. But, as we have seen, moral accountability doesn't work that way; the concept of representation interferes with and frustrates it. Thus, actions of representatives exist either alongside everyone else's and subject to the same evaluation, or they exist in a limbo beyond the grammatical reach of moral concepts—of virtue and responsibility and culpability. Moral censure of official actions, as opposed to private ones, often reflects our desire that government be our moral surrogate and responsible for what it does. The desire is understandable but futile. That would not have bothered Hobbes, but it is a continuing problem for citizens in democratic societies.

Personal Instruments

Men give themselves for hire. Their faculties are not for them, they are for those to whom they enslave themselves; their tenants are at home inside, not they.   Montaigne, "Of Husbanding your Will"

BECAUSE THEY serve the purposes of others and represent them, artificial persons are often instruments. With this in mind we call soldiers pawns of the state, the state a servant of the people, a servant the instrument of his master; similar terms are applied to lawyers.[1] Let us look at this instrumental aspect of artificial persons.

I

With artificial persons an agent's interests, concerns, and priorities are subordinated to the author's—the client or master. David Luban writes that "no genuine reciprocity exists between lawyer and client in an agency relationship: the commitment is basically a one-way street."[2] Such is the asymmetry between a person who uses and the person who is used.

---

[1] William Simon uses the expression "instrumental self," which he associates with what he calls the "psychological vision" of lawyering. In his use, "instrumental self" refers to the highly manipulative character of the legal profession, as when "the psychologists seek to assist lawyers in perfecting themselves as instruments"; "Homo Psychologicus: Notes Toward a New Legal Formalism," *Stanford Law Review* 32, 487 (Feb. 1980): 539.

[2] David Luban, *Lawyers and Justice*, (Princeton, N.J.: Princeton University Press, 1989), 326. A discussion of such asymmetrical "non-peer" relations is contained in chapter 3 of my *Equality and the Rights of Women* (Ithaca, N.Y.: Cornell University Press, 1980). Aristotle sensibly distinguishes degrees of being an instrument, between being enslaved, for instance, and being a skilled person who works in the service of others. Unlike the slave "the craftsman lives away from

Instrumental positions are common and accepted. "People often need to ask others to perform some task for them which ordinarily they would perform for themselves," writes Hanna Pitkin.[3] And a well-known handbook on agency says that "most of the world's work is performed by agents"; "the basic theory of the agency device is to enable a person, through the service of another, to broaden the scope of his activities and receive the product of another's efforts, paying such other for what he does but retaining for himself any net benefit resulting from the work performed." The key to this relation is a principal's control over his agent, a control, voluntarily acceded, "that the [agent] . . . shall act on [the principal's] . . . behalf and subject to his control." It is a deliberate fracturing of action that removes the principal from what he does. The reason is understandable: "one engaged in manufacture may well increase his productivity if he procures others to work . . . for him. By so doing, he is able to concentrate upon furnishing the ideas, the material and the supervision; the others may perform the labor."[4] Such a division of labor liberates the author from executing his plans and from dealing directly with their effects. It is absentee action.

As Oliver Wendell Holmes, Jr. said, the more we accustom ourselves to the rubric of agency, the more natural and unexceptionable the arrangement seems. But moral objections are easily found. The principal one derives from Kant, who held that treating other people as means to accomplish one's ends violates their right to respect as human beings. People should always be treated as ends in themselves, he insisted, simply because they are human. This objection needs to be reckoned with.

The agency handbook refers to another danger of the rela-

---

his employer and participates in virtue in the same measure as he participates in slavery; for the skilled mechanic is in a restricted sense in the condition of slavery"; *Politics*, trans. T. A. Sinclair, rev. Trevor J. Saunders (Harmondsworth, Eng.: Penguin, 1981), 1260a, 96.

[3] Hanna Pitkin, *The Concept of Representation* (Berkeley: University of California Press, 1967), 134.

[4] Harold Reuschlein and William Gregory, *Agency and Partnership* (St. Paul, Minn.: West Publishing Co., 1978), 1, 3. I have already remarked that these authors exclude from the class of "agents" servants as well as slaves. The reason is that servant is defined legally as "an agent employed by a master to perform service in his affairs," where the master "has the right to control the physical conduct of the other in the performance of the service"; 4. Physical control, which excludes discretionary action, is a disqualification. I use the term "agent" in an ordinary, nonlegal sense that includes servants who are sent on errands.

tionship, observing that "any human being who has the capacity to receive and . . . convey ideas, can bind another by acting as his servant or agent."[5] It is all too easy to become an agent and thus bind others. For us, however, the problem is that being an instrument of someone else violates one's own autonomy, that essential feature of being morally responsible. We have seen that autonomy requires that whatever a person does, she and no one else is in charge, she alone is responsible. Thus, insofar as artificial persons involve fractured autonomy, the Kantian objection goes to the heart of what we have already found wrong with this kind of action.

II

A lawyer needs to cultivate a certain mentality and the ability to shape his personality to the occasion in order to make himself useful. Charles Wolfram implies that some of these abilities are theatrical: "A client typically is represented by a lawyer who is expected to . . . throw himself or herself into the representation with little emotional or personal reserve. . . . American lawyers and their models [e.g., F. Lee Bailey, Percy Foreman, Melvin Belli] often perform with great investments of emotional resources."[6] Acting—pretending—is also a salient feature of business life, one writer observes, adding that "the very nature of their work numbers [business] managers among the great actors of our time."[7]

Developing such professional skills may change the professional himself; training and participation in the military profession give one "a unique perspective on the world," Samuel Huntington notes. "Those who make the military a career begin to identify themselves in terms of their role," writes Anthony Hartle, and their membership in a specialized culture makes objective analysis difficult for them. The demands on a mercenary are even tougher, argues Sir John Winthrop Hackett: "A man will suffer great inconvenience and hardship for pay . . . but the

---

[5] Ibid., 22.

[6] Charles Wolfram, "A Lawyer's Duty to Represent Clients, Repugnant and Otherwise," in David Luban, ed., *The Good Lawyer* (Totowa, N.J.: Rowman & Allanheld, 1984), 224.

[7] Robert Jackall, *Moral Mazes* (New York: Oxford University Press, 1988), 61.

cases where they will sell their own lives for cash alone are . . . exceedingly rare." The attitude required is highly specialized and fragile: "The good fighting man who honestly believes himself to be a pure mercenary in arms . . . may have to guard his convictions as vigilantly as any atheist."[8]

Different professions require different perspectives, and the narrowness of their vision is a high virtue among lawyers and military officers. A broader vision would lessen their usefulness as professional instruments, and moral criteria are understandably absent from most accounts of their professions.[9] "What adroit advocacy requires," says one legal writer, is "the ability to make a convincing case for any side in a dispute," and "moral insight may get in the way of cleverness." This applies particularly in an adversary system, where to "present the client's case in the best possible light . . . requires indifference to the moral merit of the client's interest." That unexamined interest ranks "ahead of the interests of the adversary and of third parties, as well as of public values such as justice."[10]

The lawyer puts his expertise at the client's disposal and becomes an instrument in an asymmetrical relationship of user and used. Without having specific orders like the servant, he adopts the general aim of the client as his own. In Gerald Postema's words, "the content of the lawyer's action, focused by intentions solely on the legal lever-pulling" is an action done *through* the lawyer rather than by him.[11] He shapes himself to

---

[8] Samuel Huntington, *The Soldier and the State*, (Cambridge, Mass: Harvard University Press, 1957), 60; quoted in Anthony Hartle, *Moral Issues in Military Decision Making* (Lawrence: University Press of Kansas, 1989), 36. Hartle adds that "at least this [identification of self with the position] was true in my case." Sir John Winthrop Hackett, *The Profession of Arms*, 1962 Lees Knowles Lectures, Trinity College, Cambridge (London: The Times Publishing Co., Ltd.), 14–15. Hackett reminds us of Machiavelli's distrust of mercenaries: "They are disunited, ambitious, without discipline, faithless. . . . They have no love or other motive to keep them in the field beyond a trifling wage, which is not enough to make them ready to die for you"; 15. The two characterizations are not inconsistent.

[9] It should be said, however, that Hartle and Hackett believe that moral fiber is an essential quality of good officers.

[10] Andreas Eshete, "Does a Lawyer's Character Matter?" in Luban, ed., *The Good Lawyer*, 272. Eshete's characterization resembles Plato's and Aristophanes' descriptions of the sophists, who bragged, we are told, about their ability to make the false appear true, the weaker case appear stronger, and the worse appear better.

[11] Gerald Postema, "Self-Image, Integrity, and Professional Responsibility," in Luban, ed., *The Good Lawyer*, 302.

such instrumental use. Successful business managers do something similar. Robert Jackall comments that a successful manager "dispassionately takes stock of himself, treating himself as an object, as a commodity. . . . He analyzes his strengths and weaknesses and . . . then he systematically undertakes a program to reconstruct his image, his publicly avowed attitudes or ideas. . . . This means sharply curbing one's impulses, indeed spontaneity of any sort."[12] He shapes himself to corporate usefulness and thus success.

III

To put the issue of instrumentality into relief, consider the attitude of soldiers in a citizen, nonprofessional, army. Their attitude will be predictably different from the professional's, and it may not be entirely conducive to effective fighting. One account of the Athenian army by a modern military thinker notes that "military discipline among the lively and argumentative Athenians was none too good by any standard. . . . Grosser breaches were only punished on the return of the expedition, after court cases which I imagine were usually widely enjoyed."[13] Thus, though the narrow professional perspective poses one kind of hazard, the free-thinking unprofessional perspective poses another.

However, a wider issue lurks under the surface here. While talent, acumen, judgment, and expertise are often advantages in a profession, sometimes they are burdens instead. For instance, a person of excellent artistic taste who is hired to build an ugly building or paint motel rooms may be at a disadvantage compared to others, may have difficulty doing what her client wants. Her success would be better assured, and her function better performed, if she were *less* talented and exacting. Similarly, a person of compulsive honesty, unable to dissemble,

---

[12] Jackall, *Moral Mazes*, 59. Such self-discipline and constraint—"psychic asceticism," Jackall calls it—"creates a curious sense of guilt, a regret at sustained self-abnegation and deprivation [that] finds its expression principally in one's private emotional life"; 203–4.

[13] Hackett, *Profession of Arms*, 6. Hackett adds a reminiscence: "One of my early commanding officers said sadly to me . . . 'you'll never be a soldier: you'll never be much more than an armed civilian.'" Hackett responds whimsically, "It did seem that I was in quite distinguished company."

might make a terrible salesman. "To be truthful," he might say, "you would do better to buy at the corner store." And a gourmet who works as a waiter might say of the soup when asked, "Terrible." Because of their virtues or talents, admirable in themselves, such people are ill-fitted for these jobs and don't do well in them. Their gifts clash with the requirements of their work. They could both be more successful and please their employers better if they were less discriminating or honest—which is to say, lesser in talent and virtue.

In a parallel way the law asks its practitioners to put aside issues of moral judgment; the military teaches an uncritical acceptance of orders. Similarly, the salesman is expected to avoid giving unfavorable information and to dodge uncomfortable questions. The upshot is that all these positions tend to make a person behave worse morally than he might naturally. They encourage neglect of moral constraints and moral criticism.

IV

Let us look from closer philosophical range at the relation of virtue and character to professional requirements. In the *Politics* Aristotle argues that there are—and need to be—special virtues for different social positions. He first explores this in terms of the household: there people need to fill definite roles, those of master, child, wife, and slave. Yet all humans need the particularly human virtues, Aristotle says. In that case we seem to face a paradox: "If we say that slaves have [the virtues of restraint, courage, justice, etc.], how then will they differ from free men? . . . Roughly the same question can be put in relation to wife and child." Are the virtues of these different or the same then? Aristotle recognizes there is a difficult knot here. "For if the highest excellence is required of both [ruler and ruled], why should one rule unqualifiedly, and the other unqualifiedly obey?" Moreover, "if he that rules is not to be restrained and just, how shall he rule well? And if the ruled lacks these virtues, how shall he *be* ruled well?" He concludes that "both ruler and ruled must have a share in virtue, but . . . there are differences in virtue in each case." Each must have moral virtue "not all in the same way, but only as may be required by each for his proper function." Even particular virtues have different forms: "restraint is not the same in a man as in a woman, nor justice or courage either . . . ; the one is the courage of a ruler, the other the courage of a servant, and likewise with the other virtues."[14] We are back now in the language of role moralities.

The Greek term *arete*, which is translated "virtue," was not associated with moral virtue in particular, but rather with function. An instrument has its *arete* if it works well, and a person in a certain position—slave or wife or child—needs *arete* appropriate to his or her role, the *arete* required by the role. But the ruler or husband, Aristotle says, "must have moral virtue in its entirety; for his function is in the fullest sense that of a master-craftsman" and thus requires of him rationality of the highest kind. Thus the special virtues needed in the state, and those of particular household members, are defined in terms of the larger context and "the virtue of the part . . . examined in relation to the virtue of the whole."[15]

A related point comes from Aristotle's *Nichomachean Ethics*. Having remarked that soldiering requires courage and the willingness to do what is necessary, he distinguishes the way men of virtue view it from how others do. "Death and wounds will be painful to the brave man . . . but he will face them because it is noble to do so." Some men will find this easier than others: "the more [a man] is possessed of virtue in its entirety and the happier he is, the more he will be pained at the thought of death; for life is best worth living for such a man." A nobler man, having more to lose and understanding this, has more difficulty with fighting than a person of lesser character. Aristotle con-

[14] Aristotle, *Politics*, 1259b18–1260a14, 94–95. Among the virtues peculiar to women Aristotle mentions silence.

[15] Ibid., 1260a14, 95; 1260b8, 96. Thus "both children and women must be educated with an eye to the constitution" and not with respect to some universal standard of good human development; 1260b8, 96. Martha Nussbaum, in conversation with me, objected to this point. She argued that Aristotle does not mean virtues go with the role a person takes, but rather follow from his or her nature: slaves and women have different natures; that is what determines the difference in both their roles and their virtues. But there are two objections to this. First, children don't have different natures from adults. It is their *positions*, or functions, that dictate their virtues. And Aristotle specifically speaks of the slave's role as that of a tool; 1259b, 94. Second, in referring to the whole as determining the respective virtues, Aristotle is clearly talking the language of roles. It is the larger community in which a role is embedded that determines that role's peculiar virtues. He gives a similar argument, following Plato, for the differentiated functions of parts of the soul.

cludes that "it is quite possible that the best soldiers may not be men of this sort but those who are less brave but have no other good; for these are ready to face danger, and they sell their life for trifling gains."[16] He implies that greater virtue, better character, and greater intelligence may make for lesser soldiering ability—that, in effect, greater virtue may make for lesser usefulness.

A parallel argument about lawyers is framed by Andreas Eshete. "The adversarial procedure forces lawyers to lower their sights . . . [and] withdraw their vision from the higher aims of justice . . . [focusing instead on] the humbler good ends of a client's triumph and an opponent's defeat. These aims, which would not move someone commanding an exalted perspective, draw the zeal of the person with a modest professional calling."[17] The danger of this reasoning is obvious. If the "profession" of safecracking requires a callous disregard for others' property, then that attitude is a virtue for that position. If having a cruel streak is an asset for a prison guard, then it is a virtue within that position, and so on.

But Eshete does not conclude that the needs of their positions justify moral shortsightedness in lawyers. On the contrary, he protests that "there is no good deed that can always be better accomplished by a person of less virtue." Therefore it can't be a virtue even within a profession to be a person of lesser moral virtue.[18] But if not, what should be said about the profession's requirements?

But there is another side to the issue. A restricted moral vision for lawyers is defended by Susan Wolf, who thinks that moralists should not try to reshape the system, but should

[16] Aristotle, *The Nichomachean Ethics*, trans. David Ross, J. L. Ackrill and J. O. Urmson (New York: Oxford University Press, 1980), 69–72.

[17] Eshete, "Does a Lawyer's Character Matter?" 277. The price of this dedication is not negligible, Eshete continues, for "the lawyer living up to his adversarial station is . . . in a [bad] predicament. In doing what is required, he would be undertaking morally questionable acts and acquiring unattractive traits of character; and this . . . would be good grounds for moral regret"; 279.

[18] Ibid., 278. It should be noticed that Aristotle didn't say it was a *virtue* to be possessed of lesser virtue, even in a profession where less virtue was better than more. But it does put him in a curious position. If the cultivation of less virtuous attitudes is important for the skills of a profession, what of the moral justification of the profession? Aristotle believed with Plato that the state should encourage the moral development of its citizens.

worry about allowing lawyers "to fulfill the role to which the present legal system assigns them in a way that maximally contributes to the achievement of the goals for which the system is designed." Her thinking is framed by the present shape and function of the profession: "If lawyers were to model their professional selves according to an ideal that consistently made the promotion of truth and justice the direct, overriding aim, it would make no sense for persons to contract the services of a lawyer." It would undermine the profession.[19]

V

Given their effects on character, should conscientious people avoid such hazardous professions? Gerald Postema answers no, but adds that the responsible person who chooses such a profession will need to "integrate [morally problematic] actions and the professional commitments that call for them into a coherent conception of his or her moral life. He or she must be able to justify . . . the decisions made and the actions taken by reference to this general conception, while accepting responsibility for the sacrifice of conflicting moral concerns."[20]

Andreas Eshete disagrees, arguing that such a conception means "lawyers must adopt a rather strange attitude toward their work: they must see what they do professionally as a form of acting," and as a result, "character is screened from professional conduct."[21] This resembles Montaigne's solution to the question of how to live with oneself and avoid schizophrenia. A person "integrates" himself by effectually compartmentalizing roles and personal life; then the two coexist side by side without conflict.[22] It is the old problem of the insulation of roles from moral criticism.

[19] Susan Wolf, "Ethics, Legal Ethics, and the Ethics of Law," in Luban, ed., *The Good Lawyer*, 48–49. Wolf thinks there is a moral constraint in the idea of a good lawyer: "the moral constraint still applies to the person who *is* a lawyer; it simply has no bearing on our evaluation of this person's quality *as* a lawyer"; 50.

[20] Gerald Postema, "Self-Image, Integrity, and Professional Responsibility," in Luban, ed., *The Good Lawyer*, 289.

[21] Eshete, "Does a Lawyer's Character Matter?" 276.

[22] Anthony Hartle also thinks that fitting together is needed in the military profession, since the ethic of professionals does not simply supersede ordinary morality. How this fitting together can be done, considering the military's emphasis on actions that are both immoral and illegal outside the profession, is left unclear.

The ability to separate one's working self from one's personal life is called "doubling" by Robert Lifton, who applies it to some doctors at Auschwitz. They did not think of themselves as doing the selections, but put such actions at a distance. They responded, he says, to an "implicit command to bring forth a self that could adapt to killing without one's feeling oneself a murderer." Lifton says this also happened in other less grotesque medical situations: "Doubling usually begins with the student's encounter with the corpse he or she must dissect. . . . One feels it necessary to develop a 'medical self,' which enables one not only to be relatively inured to death but to function reasonably efficiently in relation to the many-sided demands of the work."[23] The distinction applies to the brutal Mengele, of whom a colleague said that "he had all the sentimental notions, all the human feelings, pity, and so on. But there was in his psyche a hermetically closed cell, impenetrable, indestructible cell, which is obedience to the received order." Lifton comments that "the ideal doctor . . . remains warm and humane by keeping that doubling to a minimum."[24]

Soldiers in a theater of action also inure themselves to the awful consequences of their actions and expertise, and various kinds of propaganda, rhetoric, and innocent-sounding euphemisms help them. But in the end a sense of personal detachment from the action may be most necessary.[25] Physical distance, as in bombing, helps alleviate the moral problem of killing civilians precisely by preventing a soldier from seeing the effects of his actions. The psychological distance of doubling serves a similar purpose.

But however urgently invoked, the strategy of separation may not always work, as Postema observes. "Even the most detached lawyer will feel pride, or a sense of fulfillment or frustration" at his performance in the role and "to feel such emotions, one must identify with their objects; they must be seen as . . .

[23]Robert Jay Lifton, *The Nazi Doctors* (New York: Basic Books, 1986), 425, 426–27, 427. Lifton writes of one doctor who wrestled with his position in the camp, he "wanted to see his wife and children . . . but was aware of a feeling of guilt . . . [and] felt the need to keep his wife and Auschwitz separate"; 319.

[24]Ibid., 375, 427.

[25]Regarding the demands put on the military psyche, see Richard Gabriel, *No More Heroes: Madness and Psychiatry in War* (New York: Hill and Wang, 1987) and *The Painful Field* (Westport, Conn.: Greenwood Press, 1988). Gabriel argues that the stresses of modern war may surpass the abilities of people to deal with them.

reflecting in some important way on oneself."[26] The urge to see oneself as the person who performs well is irresistible. Thus, separating self from role requires a context where someone can *both* be proud of what she does and not feel responsible for it. But Postema, like Eshete, doesn't think such separation is salutary. He tries to integrate them, saying that "morally responsible action in professional roles calls for a fully engaged and robust faculty of moral judgment, a willingness to identify with the consequences of one's actions and take responsibility for them."[27] He does not concede that professional requirements are necessarily at odds with morality, yet his integration thesis is not wholly convincing.

VI

Using a person as an instrument seems at first no more problematic than using a long stick to get something out of reach.[28] It provides a way of increasing one's personal efficacy in the world and enlarging one's sphere of action. With such instruments a person can effectively be in several places at once and can do things impossible to do alone. Thus, instrumental people are attractive aids to a complicated life or business; they serve to create wonderful creatures with many arms and legs which are able to act at large distances from a single center. They participate in making figures of great and extended power with widely various talents and skills—complex, ubiquitous Superpersons with superhuman capabilities.[29]

[26] Postema, "Self-Image," 301. A firsthand account of one man's struggle with the demands of the legal profession is reported by Studs Terkel. A lawyer recounts how, having found the tension between his values and his work unbearable, he proceeded to work only with powerless and indigent clients. "My work and my life, they've become one. No longer am I schizophrenic," he writes; Terkel, *Working* (New York: Random House, 1986), 539.

[27] Postema, "Self-Image," 310.

[28] Hanna Pitkin speaks of an agent as "a tool or instrument by which the other acts," and distinguishes agents from representatives through the latter's more substantial position; *Concept of Representation*, 125. Her remarks reflect the asymmetry of the master-servant paradigm.

[29] The idea of extending one's personal power through agents is familiar in law; e.g., Postema observes that "the lawyer becomes an extension of the legal, and to an extent the moral, personality of the client"; "Moral Responsibility in Professional Ethics," *New York University Law Review* 55, 1 (Apr. 1980): 77. The attractiveness of such extension of power is confirmed by the relish with which

But when things are done at such a distance, the individual author is detached from the reality she manipulates and from the people who extend her presence, her metaphorical arms and legs.[30] Although she may see the situation as a simple two-party contractual relation entered into voluntarily, this is inadequate for a moral account. For one thing, it ignores those who must deal with the author's spokespersons rather than with her. There is a great potential for confusion about intentions and underlying assumptions, and the dealings have an impersonal quality that stems from the author's absence. There is the understandable temptation to treat the absentee author as if she were not a person at all, as if she were an impersonal entity. These ramifications invite moral problems.[31]

Consider the matter this way. An artificial person or agent does not see what is done as his own action, strictly speaking; nor can he see it precisely as the author does. To exercise judgment in his position he needs a perspective that is neither his own nor the author's, but a third, which combines his actions and expertise with the author's purposes. Adopting such a view is a sophisticated and imaginative move, requiring at once detachment and involvement—detachment from oneself and involvement with the fictional person's success and appearance in the eyes of others.

Of course, the taking of such an imaginary perspective, like the doubling of doctors, involves some alienation from oneself and one's moral beliefs, one's purposes, self-respect, and affiliations. It means treating oneself, not as a full-fledged end, but as an instrument to be used in the construction of a superbeing that is both more and less than a human. The action too is changed, and as R. F. Holland says in a different connection,

---

stories of empire builders are recounted—as, recently, about Donald Trump. I discuss the moral aspect of such superhuman figures in *The Grammar of Justice*, 165–66.

[30] A colorful and whimsical portrayal of this kind of detachment is given by Gabriel Garcia Marquez in *The Autumn of the Patriarch* (1976).

[31] Negotiations done in the name of someone absent have a queer impersonality for both negotiators. The absence of one of the central persons makes it difficult to see how ordinary moral rules apply. It is unsurprising, then, to hear that white-collar thieves and shoplifters often do not think that they steal *from someone*, from some identifiable person; they steal from a company, a government department, an institution. The absence of a personal relationship between the parties fosters the sense that ordinary moral standards do not hold.

one "becomes . . . an instrument: as though in principle there could have been something else—a piece of wire there instead." The action's character as *human* is in jeopardy; "human agents could disappear and robots take their place without diminishing by one iota the prevailing amount of 'moral' value."[32]

Now an instrument is an inanimate object with a use, like a stick, and such things lack moral significance. Aristotle provides the paradigm of a human instrument: "a slave is a sort of living piece of property; and like any other servant is a tool in charge of other [inanimate] tools."[33] This paradigm, which is fundamental to the theory of legal agency, is a harsh one to apply to respected professionals in law, government, and the military. Yet its source lies in the theory of agency, as we have seen. Despite that, people in those professions serve voluntarily and are proud of their commitment to service and honor, and of their expertise; witness the soldier's willingness to lay down his life for his country. Seen this way, service as an instrument may seem to merit an even higher degree of respect than other occupations do.

The pride of lawyers in making themselves useful and exerting themselves on behalf of strangers' causes appears to be misplaced, however, when considered morally. One's pride in what one can be used for neglects the respect that is owing to oneself. Offering oneself to be used by others is thus analogous to prostitution.

Another objection to the arrangement comes from the side of the author. It is ironic, but the personal instruments who so enhance a person's capabilities and expand her efficacy work to diminish the author morally. For the privilege of acting at a distance is purchased at a cost, in that these actions are not intrinsically personal to her; in them she is replaceable by a surrogate. And the assumption that the actions will be the same whether she or someone else does them undermines the moral respect one should have for one's self. She must view her actions as if she is a figurehead, having merely formal relation to them. A further cost is the loss of that respect for her personal presence

[32] R. F. Holland, *Against Empiricism* (Totowa, N.J.: Barnes & Noble, 1980), 115. Holland is arguing against Henrik von Wright and the utilitarians, but his protest against detaching action from its agent reflects the point I am making.

[33] *Politics*, 1253b, 64–65.

that belongs to dealing with others directly, for such direct dealing involves ways of showing respect and receiving it.[34] She becomes instead a shadow figure in these—her own—transactions.

The arrangement wears an innocent face and appears in countless forms in modern life. An employer hires someone to act as his agent and thinks this unproblematic, as unproblematic as if he took the same actions himself. He hires someone who is willing to do what he would do, had he time and ability. But that does not redeem the instrumental use; others cannot be used as one's surrogate without diminishing their autonomy, which is to say their moral status, and without diminishing one's own claim to respect. Let us explore this latter aspect further.

VII

Putting oneself in the service of someone else requires deference, an attitude that troubles Thomas Hill. "To be servile," he writes, "is . . . to have a certain attitude concerning one's rightful place in a moral community." He asks whether there are moral arguments against having such an attitude. Suppose a person doesn't object to putting himself at the service of another, is even proud of doing it? "It is not . . . obviously wrong to demand less for oneself than one deserves," he notes. Yet something is morally amiss; either there is "a failure to understand and acknowledge one's own moral rights," or, if one understands them, one wrongly accepts and approves their violation. "A black who plays the Uncle Tom [is] . . . displaying disregard for his own moral position as an equal among human beings. Similarly a woman throws away her rights too lightly if she continues to play the subservient role because she is used to it or is too timid to risk a change." Hill thinks these people exemplify "a willingness to disavow one's moral status, publicly

---

[34] The loss of respect for self on the side of such authors is suggested by the fact that many magnates of politics and business tend to use themselves impersonally, to "drive themselves" to accomplish impersonal ends, and thus neglect their personal lives. Francis Bacon remarked that "men in great place are thrice servants—servants of the sovereign or state, servants of fame, and servants of business; so as they have no freedom neither in their persons, nor in their actions, nor in their times"; "Of Great Place," in Bacon, *Essays and New Atlantis* (New York: Van Nostrand Co., 1942), 42.

and systematically, in the absence of any strong reason to do so."
It is the inverse of arrogance: "an arrogant person ignores the
rights of others, thereby arrogating for himself a higher status
than he is entitled to; a servile person denies his own rights,
thereby assuming a lower position than he is entitled to." Both
are wrong.[35]

Every person ought to respect his own moral worth as part of
respecting morality itself, Hill argues. "A person who fully respected a system of moral rights would be disposed to learn his
proper place in it, to affirm it proudly, and not to tolerate abuses
of it lightly. This is just the sort of disposition that the servile
person lacks." Therefore "to the extent that a person gives even
tacit consent to humiliations incompatible with [the respect that
belongs to him as a human], he will be acting as if he waives a
right which he cannot in fact give up."[36]

Much of Hill's argument can be applied to lawyers, military
personnel, corporate middlemen, and other artificial persons.
Professionalism and institutionalized work arrangements support the use of willing instruments, and they support it on both
sides. On the author's side there seems no reason to forbear
using sanctioned and respectable instruments; and from the
side of the instrument, sanction is given to a profession where
one can help others and one's expertise is highly valued.

One defense of these professions can be anticipated: of
course military people must be ready to kill and destroy, lawyers
must be ready to misrepresent and deceive, and corporate officials must be ready to cut favorable deals. But while these jobs
are unsavory, so are many other jobs, like collecting garbage or
arresting criminals. But they may be necessary. Therefore, like
these other unpleasant positions, the professions under discussion must be tolerated, even though they are morally distasteful.

But such analogies as these are mistaken. What is wrong with
the professions we are considering is not any unpleasant quality
of the work, but the moral relation in which the work requires

[35] Thomas Hill, "Servility and Self-Respect," *The Monist* 57, 1 (Jan. 1973): 90,
92, 93, 95, 96. Hill is concerned chiefly with the place and attitude of women and
blacks. He thinks that some dire threat to oneself or to another might justify a
deferential attitude, while "a small profit" would not; 96. What about a large
profit? My argument implies that it too would fail to justify what Hill characterizes as a moral wrong.
[36] Ibid., 99, 101–2.

these people to stand to others, and to themselves. And the necessity for them needs to be shown, not assumed.

VIII

The acceptability of persons serving as instruments pervades whole disciplines and fields—economics, business management, social theory, to mention a few. Malthus and Keynes, in their different times, spoke of labor as a resource and of workers as interchangeable units filling a specialized function in a mechanical productive system. The language persists today: labor is a requirement of production like capital and raw materials, and its cost must be bargained for like these others. As a resource, labor has its requirements for existence; thus Malthus speaks of material necessities of life as enabling workers to produce and reproduce, as if he were talking about a machine's fuel and maintenance. That perspective recurs in a somewhat softened form in later economists to whom labor and its use, like the use of other materials of production, is morally neutral. Insofar as human services are part of production, they must be budgeted for, evaluated for efficiency, pruned when the market lags, and discarded when unproductive.

Supporting this view of workers is a matter-of-fact scientific emphasis on the economics of production. Just as business has its specialized function, the workers have theirs; all are pieces of a large and complex economic machine where human values are anomalous. In consequence, business separates itself from the human beings in it by means of a conceptual barrier, a mechanical economic model. The model provides an amoral context to thinking and reasoning about human participants, a context that is devoid of human relationships and obligations.

This depersonalization extends even wider. In economics, the family appears as a unit with specific functions—with income, demographic features, and spending habits. And the nation is made up of such entities; all can be dealt with for social and economic purposes without using any language that would trigger moral inferences. Thus, thanks to this framework, economics and much social theory, albeit unwittingly, sanction the dehumanization of persons and the neglect of them as moral entities. One can easily understand in this light Marx's protest against materialism and the degrading of workers, their forced "alienation" both from the products of their labor and from themselves. Sciences like economics and business management, whose subjects essentially deal with the stuff of morality, manage thus to exclude moral considerations.

We see that our complex social institutions depend on instrumental persons in countless ways, both directly and through institutions. Viewed casually, as we saw, paying other people to do one's work seems like a simple, voluntary, contractual arrangement. In the end (one says) it's work like any other work. But this last is false. Work done in instrumental positions is fundamentally different, morally different, from work done even partly through one's own initiative and decision. Yet given the variety of ways that such positions are cast in our institutions, their moral hazard seems both pervasive and inescapable.

EIGHT

Persons in Context

There are intimate conceptual connections between the possible ways in which individuals may live their lives and the institutions of society.

Peter Winch, *Ethics and Action*

USING AN AGENT severs a person from her actions. She is in a sense not present, either physically absent or refusing to participate in actions that are attributable to her. In consequence, artificial persons strain the terms that are used to describe actions. Let us test this against some common philosophical claims about action and responsibility. Here I shall not use "agent" in the legal sense, but as philosophers commonly do, to mean simply a person who acts or can act.

I

In most accounts of action, it is crucial that a person *causes* what is attributed to him, causes it in something like the sense that a natural force causes something, as rain causes a pond to fill. A person is normally the cause of his voluntary activity; and when he is not, then *he* did not do whatever happened. "Unless an agent is the ultimate cause of a given item of his behavior, then that behavior is no action of his, it being one and the same thing to say that a given man does something and that he causes it to happen."[1] How does this description fit artificial persons? There

[1] Richard Taylor, *Action and Purpose* (Englewood Cliffs, N.J.: Prentice-Hall, 1966), 120. However, Taylor adds that physical causation differs conceptually from the causation of agency; 138. Donald Davidson agrees that "causality is central to the concept of agency" but claims that "it is ordinary causality between events that is relevant," not a special kind of cause; *Essays on Actions and Events* (London: Oxford University Press, 1980), 53. Also see Roderick Chisholm, *Person and Object* (Peru, Ill.: Open Court, 1979), ch. 2

two (or more) persons are causally involved and asymmetrically cause what happens. Thus, if causality is required to identify an agent, then two-person actions mean that any identification of an agent will be muddied. Stressing a causal relation underscores the problematic nature of artificial persons.

Action theory requires that actions have identifiable agents, but with artificial persons it is not, as D. G. Brown says, truistic that "any kind of action will be some kind of doing on the part of an agent."[2] There may be no agent, strictly speaking, or several. We can only say that it is some kind of doing. But need we assume that an action must have an agent? If not, then it would be unproblematic that many actions have none.[3] That would fit the modern situation neatly and dispose of the moral problem *tout court*: nobody is responsible because nobody acts.

Still another central feature of action is intention: to have done an action, one must have *intended* to do it "under some description," Donald Davidson says.[4] This dresses the ambiguities in new clothes. The author of an action intends a particular end, but the actor also intends what she does, perhaps under a different description; both act intentionally. This leads to the two-action dilemma. However, the description of what they are doing may be the same; for instance, each of them can be said to be buying a property, or fighting a war, or running a business; yet their participation differs in significant and troublesome ways. The effort to identify intentions as a key to locating responsibility fails in the same way that identifying an agent failed.

It is often held that an agent must be *free* to be responsible for what she does.[5] Responsible action is action that *could have been done* differently. This condition is often considered crucial: where an agent is not free, her responsibility is at best qualified. But is it the author or the actor who must be free? And what does freedom mean for the artificial person *once engaged to represent an author*? That is one aspect of the problem we're trying to clarify. Another aspect is this: if *both* parties must be free, are we

[2] D. G. Brown, *Action* (Toronto: University of Toronto Press, 1968), 111.

[3] See Aubrey Castell, *The Self in Philosophy* (London: Macmillan, 1965), ch. 3, for a discussion of characteristic views on the question whether an action must have an agent.

[4] Davidson, *Actions and Events*, 50.

[5] See Castell, *Self in Philosophy*, ch. 4.

speaking about freedom with respect to two actions or only one?[6] We return to the old puzzle.

What, furthermore, does it mean to say that a committee action could have been done differently? Does it means that each or some of the committee members might have voted differently? But then we are considering many actions, *each* of which must be free, and then the unity of the agent is forfeit. This question exposes familiar problems: the committee doesn't have free will except in the sense that individuals comprising it might have voted differently, but at the same time, it isn't the individuals who are the agent.

Thus traditional accounts of persons' actions and their moral import are unhelpful in dealing with artificial persons. Instead, these accounts uncover and founder on the same problems we have seen before. The conceptual analyses even become part of the practical dilemmas concerning responsibility, for their crisp terms are inapplicable to the ambiguous artificial persons, and thus they leave the central notion of moral agency inapplicable in this important area.

In general the ambiguities associated with artificial persons work infectiously, spreading to all the terms normally associated with action and responsibility, and thus defying clarification. These odd persons strain the fabric and vocabulary of moral theory, just as they frustrate common-sense demands. The underlying reason, as I have argued, is the dissonance between the moral paradigm and the contexts that artificial persons create, a dissonance that seems incorrigible.

II

Different views about people's relation to jobs and institutions may contain different conceptions of a person; conversely, different conceptions of person dictate different views of institutions. The Kantian individual legislates for himself, without consideration for personal affections, others' dependency on him, or the

[6]John Chipman Gray makes will central to the legal meaning of "person" because a person "is a subject of legal rights and duties," and "to give effect to a man's right, an exercise of free will on his part is necessary"; *The Nature and Sources of the Law*, 2nd ed., (New York: Macmillan, 1931), 27, 23. The problem here is that we have two parties but provision for only one will.

felt particulars of his life—his bonds and emotional attachments, for instance. He stands above these and consults rational
principles that would apply to anyone in his situation, regardless of personal differences. That is an aspect of his freedom as
well; nothing binds his choice about which principles are relevant. And from this lofty detachment he applies his choice of
action universally.

Distance from the exigencies of human life also characterizes
the individual in John Rawls's "original position," a standpoint
from which everyone's choices are cast under the same, impersonal conditions. In that position people are assumed to be ignorant of who they are, and thus they choose the rules of the
society from an abstract, hypothetical framework. But such a requirement of impersonality and interchangeability excludes
much that ordinary moral reasoning must consider, questions
about which obligations and needs have priority among the
many demands and bonds of one's life. The assumption of ignorance forces an abstraction on people who, even from birth,
are destined to balance very different moral claims.[7] The hypothetical position is too lean for serious moral inferences.

In contrast to Rawls's, the individual of my argument operates in a context of moral particulars. She has a background of
relations, her family and other commitments, which will not reflect the situation of most others. For any individual, the obligations of employment and profession have some claim to respect,
but none are absolute, and they exist side by side with other
demands. All these considerations affect my individual, and
only from the center of them can she legislate for herself in a
morally responsible way. Her legislation will thus lack the generality of Kant or Rawls.[8] Then, is she autonomous or not? In
Kant's sense she is not, for her decisions are not abstractly based
or universalizable; some go back into her past or reach widely
into the lives of those around her. Their universalization would

---

[7] W. H. Walsh says that "it is naive to suppose that human beings act in total
isolation from their fellows," and protests that moral theory overemphasizes individual responsibility; "Pride, Shame, and Responsibility," *Philosophical Quar-
terly* 20, 78 (Jan. 1970): 8. I am protesting the other side, that our institutions are
at odds with our moral requirements.

[8] Peter Winch argues in general against the universalizability of moral judgments, proposing that the perspective of each person affects the question what
is right as he is faced with it; "The Universalizability of Moral Judgments," in
Winch, *Ethics and Action* (London: Routledge & Kegan Paul, 1972).

be meaningless. Yet insofar as she makes her decisions as a rational person who weighs all the aspects for herself, she exercises autonomy in a different sense from Kant's. She makes decisions in a web of opposing demands; she balances, adjusts tensions, tries to be consistent, looks for stable arrangements. Her decisions are, in a very exacting and personal sense, hers.

To see this in perspective, consider a very different theoretical individual that contrasts to both Kant's and mine; it is posited by Roberto Unger. Unger commends roles because they "seem to guarantee the unity of the self by providing a person with a social place. . . . Each role helps its occupants picture the continuity of their lives and the ties of common humanity that bind them to their fellows. In exchange for doing what is expected of you, you will be rewarded by other men's opinion" that what you're doing is rational, understandable to them. "It is just what you need to feel safe in the possession of a continuous self." Unger's vulnerable self seeks security in the advantages of roles and accepts an implicit contract with his society. He will fill the role, and in turn the community will accept and not threaten him. He becomes like others: "Many men are in it besides yourself. You will naturally come to have interests and inclinations in common with them. It will not take you long to recognize that in many respects you are like the others." As "recurring positions," such roles require departures from how one would act otherwise. Thus, Unger says, "in the role the public and the private aspects of the self are kept apart. The more the external conventions of a role are accepted, the less does the private self exist." For an individual to depart from his role is hazardous, Unger argues: "The more freedom one achieves from the constraints of these conventions, the less he finds support for his sense of the temporal unity and social character of the self." Thus people are victim to insecurity and disintegration on the one side, and on the other, "to the extent they sacrifice the private self to the public one, they surrender their individual identities."[9] But Unger thinks the surrender is rightly made. On balance, roles and the conformity they require perform an important function for humans, mainly by connecting them in social wholes and showing individuals their similarities to one another.

Unger's individual shows a particular set of traits. In contrast

[9]Roberto Unger, *Knowledge and Politics* (New York: Macmillan, 1975), 60–62.

to mine, he cheerfully trades independent judgment for social acceptance, autonomy for security. For such an individual the artificial-person arrangement, with its ambiguities, is in harmony with his world and untroubling. This figure is also strikingly different from Kant's model, which can be seen as one extreme on a spectrum that has Unger's at the other end. My individual, with her qualified autonomy, stands somewhere between the two; not detached from the restrictions of relations, affections, and commitments, but able to choose within the bounds of these without being governed either by abstract principles or the authority of roles. Consequently she risks the social disapproval that drives Unger's individual to conform.[10] Notice that each of these figures has its appropriate social setting. Unger's needs a highly structured environment where he knows at each turn what to do and is not punished for the consequences. Kant's needs wide freedom to act on his principles, regardless of how his actions affect others. He needs a context where praise follows motives and principles only, never the consequence. Unlike both of these, my figure needs an environment that values individual authority and responsibility, one where institutions do not thwart or obscure these, and one where the personal bonds that restrict a person's choices are respected. A certain kind of individual inhabits a given context, and a conception of person is embedded in a given social fabric.

What I am arguing, of course, is that person and society must be seen as synergistic, that modifications of the one affect the other. From this the inference is unavoidable that a careful critique of our institutions is in order if we want an appropriate setting for morally responsible people. Others have noticed the connection between our morals and our institutions. Robert Jackall argued that business managers' "conservative public style and conventional demeanor hide their transforming role in our society." He believes "they are the principal carriers of the bureaucratic ethic in our era. . . . Their occupations, ethics and the way they come to see the world set both the frameworks and

---

[10]These three figures can be compared with John Stuart Mill's in *On Liberty*. Mill's person is sensitive to public pressure and often will conform at the price of his creativity and ability to innovate, rather than risk public disapproval. Given such an individual, Mill appeals to "society" for generous toleration, partly on grounds of individual worth, partly for the long-term social benefit.

the vocabularies for a great many public issues in our society," and help to shape "actual morality in our society as a whole."[11] It is a plausible and troubling contention.

III

An alternative to institutional change may, even here, seem available. For if there is dissonance between traditional morality and modern arrangements and institutions, may it not be due to the stringency of our moral concepts themselves—those of action and person, autonomy and responsibility? These, with their one-person paradigm and its limitations, simply fail to apply to much that humans do in a modern setting. Thus, what we need are not different institutions but different concepts, ones that better fit the institutions and social structure we have. We should criticize moral standards themselves and substitute more modern concepts for outdated ones fitted to a simpler entrepreneurial society. We should change our moral language rather than turn the social clock backwards.

Take fragmented action. Instead of criticizing this form of action and trying to introduce unity, we could reinterpret moral responsibility. We could tailor responsibility to fit the troublesome artificial persons in their modern manifestations. The old meaning of personal responsibility would no longer apply; instead we would locate responsibility some other way—perhaps by assigning it to whole groups or organizations, rather than to single individuals. Outdated moral concepts are the heart of the problem, not institutions.

Let us look at this proposal. The meaning of liability varies with different cultures, says anthropologist Klaus-Friedrich Koch. It can mean "an individual obligation and lie only with the person who is held to have caused an injury . . . or a collective obligation and fall on that person and/or other people by virtue of their association with one another." Unlike individual liability, "joint liability is an obligation to render compensation or to suffer punishment that is shared by the liable party and other individual members from among his group." He gives as

[11] Robert Jackall, *Moral Mazes* (New York: Oxford University Press, 1988), 12–13. This view is echoed in Nancy Schwartz's view of the communitarian leader in *The Blue Guitar* (Chicago: University of Chicago Press, 1988).

an example the Nazi *Sippenhaft* law we encountered in Chapter 2, "which subjected family members of a person charged with political offense to punitive measures."[12] Vicarious liability is exemplified by the familiar idea that parents should make good any damage caused by their minor child.

The meanings of other moral terms will change with a change in the meaning of liability. The *cause* of an injury will not matter much, and *intentions* may be irrelevant. For instance, the Yurok Indians of California hold that, "in the case of a house burning down while its owner ferries someone across a river, the passenger is liable for the damage because the ferryman might have extinguished the fire and saved his house had he not provided the service," a service he is obliged to perform. It is not (in our sense) the passenger's *fault*; nonetheless he is liable. Another example: the law of the Jalē in New Guinea "does not distinguish between intent, mistake, negligence, and accident" as they bear on an action, writes Koch. "In evaluating only the consequences of an act, the Jalē do not question a person's culpability when they establish his formal liability" and determine whether he must pay compensation. The connection between these concepts is reversed: guilt *follows from* liability instead of determining it.

Prompted by these different practices, we might imagine that someone who fulfills her institutional or public role has no moral responsibility for her actions. As with Unger's hypothetical contract between the person and the society, so long as she fulfills her role, society will support her. She is not expected to judge the rightness of her actions or criticize its institutions. If she commits an offense through performing her role, the institution or organization and everyone in it might be held liable, but she will not be liable in particular. Similarly, all the members of a corporation might be liable for what one person does, not because they individually contributed to or knew about the misdeed, but simply because they were members of the organization. That is similar to the way a whole family shares the liability of a Jalē offender; all have to pay for his offense.[13] Needless to

---

[12] Klaus-Friedrich Koch, "Liability and Social Structure," in Donald Black, ed., *Toward a General Theory of Social Control* (Orlando, Fla: Academic Press, 1984), 98.

[13] Ibid., 120, 107. On the Yurok, Koch cites as his source A. L. Kroeber, "The Yurok: Law and Custom," in *Handbook of the Indians of California*, Smithsonian

say, this would drastically change the way corporate actions are viewed by stockholders as well as officers.

Among the Jalē there is no strict dividing line between persons in the family, no distinction with respect to responsibility, and no concept of autonomy. A person is identified with his family and they with him. Introduced into a modern context, this arrangement would allow for complaints of injury and insult; it allows for censure and punishments, blame and guilt, and the teaching of what is acceptable, and so on. But the censure and guilt would not pertain to individuals except as they belonged to a group, and the group would be liable for damages and would accept censure for what an individual did. In that setting, people would not be presumed to have control over the actions they were responsible for or control over their consequences.[14]

The system of the Jalē locates moral accountability for wrongdoing, and does it unequivocally. But for us to adopt it would require a dramatic adjustment in our idea of responsibility. Like *Sippenhaft* and group or community reparations, this system im-

---

Institution Bureau of American Ethnology, Bull. 78 (1925). He describes this case from the Jalē. "A man became liable for the death of a woman and her child despite his efforts to prevent the fatal accident. He was cutting down a large branch of a tree that grew close to a path when the woman approached. Disregarding both the markings that he had placed across the path to warn people of the danger and his furious shouts, the woman hurried on. As she passed the tree, the branch broke and killed her and the child she was carrying on her shoulders." The woman's kinsmen were entitled to indemnification because "the branch fell down by his hands," even though the accident occurred "through the woman's own fault"; 107–8. Similar customs hold in tribes of Africa, where liability and responsibility are also collective rather than individual; see A. N. Allott, "Legal Personality in African Law," and M. Gluckman, "Property Rights and Status in African Traditional Law," both in Max Gluckman, ed., *Ideas and Procedures in African Customary Law* (London: Oxford University Press, 1969). It needs to be noticed that Koch doesn't speak, as I do, about *moral* responsibility but only liability, which has a more legalistic connotation. Nonetheless, we would interpret a custom of punishing or penalizing an individual, or his family or village, for an identifiable pattern of action as moral censuring. We would be inclined to say that the Jalē hold a person's family morally accountable for his misdeeds.

[14] Among the Gururumba people of New Guinea, there was an accepted way of denying that one was in control. By acting "like a wild pig," a man could show that he could not cope with his responsibilities, and so long as he acted that way, he was treated as possessed and not responsible; Philip Newman, "'Wild Man' Behavior in a New Guinea Highlands Community," *American Anthropologist* 66, 1 (Feb. 1964): 1–19. When a "wild man" returned to normal, he was not punished for misdeeds done during that time, as if he were assumed to be helpless to control himself.

poses punishment on (what we call) innocent or non-offending people.[15] To accept this would require us to change not only our moral practices and institutions, but, most important, our moral intuitions and the language that goes with them. Such a revised moral system, employing different concepts under familiar names, has no power to satisfy our moral demands, which is to say, our present demands. We object to *Sippenhaft* because it unfairly penalizes whole families for the behavior of their military member. And we object to punitive measures taken against whole villages as punishment for one member's offense. Both kinds of action punish many who are innocent.[16] Without some direct causal connection with a deed, it seems wrong to hold a person morally responsible; that is a simple truth according to our reasoning. A person's family are not in control of him, he is in control of himself, which is to say, he acts autonomously.

W. H. Walsh might protest here that we already practice group responsibility and feel guilt by association, and these are necessary aspects of existence in a social setting. "The fortunes of my family are my fortunes, whether I like it or not, and regardless of what I do or do not do about it." And we feel guilt and shame as a result, guilt for things we had and have no control over: "Few of us even now would regard with total indifference the revelation that, say, his father had been a notorious swindler . . . that we were directly related to Hitler, Quisling or even the Marquis de Sade."[17] But Walsh might not assimilate this kind of case to the situations described above. I agree that our relations to others determine many duties without our choice. But in our culture, responsibility for a father's misdeeds, for instance, lacks palpable form. We are not blamed for them, nor held liable for them and, if we were, would find it unfair.

The hope of revising our moral concepts to fit present facts

[15]The objection is sometimes made against affirmative-action policies that they punish the innocent. This suggests that it is important to ground affirmative action differently, perhaps in the need for greater diversity in various educational, work, and professional contexts.

[16]Our insistence on presuming a person on trial to be innocent reflects our abhorrence of punishing someone for something he didn't do.

[17]Walsh, "Pride, Shame, and Responsibility," 11. He argues that since we already feel responsibility, shame, and pride in actions we had no control over, moral theory needs to be revised to reflect this reality of moral life. Interestingly, some of his examples of group shame or guilt, especially those connected with government, are explained by my analysis of artificial person.

fails to confront the reason that the issue has any importance to begin with. Our objection to professional and institutional irresponsibility comes from a belief that *someone* is responsible, and this belief springs from our appreciation of moral standards. Without that moral understanding, there would be no problem: we would simply accept the fact that countless professional and institutional contexts are responsibility-free. And if we were like the Jalē, we would find guilt by association perfectly acceptable, not hesitating to prosecute a person for the wrongs of his agent.[18] But our understanding of moral behavior and responsibility is tied to different concepts and different demands.

The framework in which the problems about artificial persons are raised—that of our moral concepts and training—is also where the solutions need to be framed. The vocabulary in which the question is asked is the one where its answer has to be couched. In the framework of moral discourse, *our* moral discourse, individual responsibility needs to take recognizable form in such answers. Attributing group liability for an individual's offense is not among our options then. We cannot escape confronting our institutions through the device of linguistic manipulation.

IV

Social thinkers make various assumptions about human nature. Hobbes thought that by nature people are independent and self-motivated, that they compete with each other continually to gain their desires, and that they need external restraints to bring peace and order. This view forms the background for his social theory; and one can find these same assumptions echoed in many modern writers, who believe that human nature is a basic and unalterable given from which social institutions derive and which they ought to fit. We make our institutions and can shape them; legal institutions are said to be "made for humans and by humans, not humans for or by" them.[19] The task is to design institutions fitting to human nature.

---

[18] One of the objections to French's proposal (discussed in Chapter 5) to make both individuals and corporations responsible for wrongdoing was the unnaturalness of attributing character to a corporation. While that is our perception, it might not be the Jalēs'.

[19] Neil MacCormick, *An Institutional Theory of Law* (Dordrecht, Holland: D. Reidel, 1986), 67.

But another way to see people and their institutions comes from George Herbert Mead: he held that a person is inseparable from her society, that it both shapes her and depends on her support. A self does not precede social experience, but develops out of it, he thought. We incorporate attitudes of others into ourselves as we learn from childhood to play various parts. "A person is a personality because he belongs to a community, because he takes over the institutions of the community into his own conduct," and internalizes the community's standards. "Selves can only exist in definite relationships to other selves."[20] There is no set of irreducible human entities, natural persons from which a society is made; instead society provides the stuff from which a recognizable self is formed.

Since we acquire relationships and roles in society, some of them involuntarily, Mead reasons that interpersonal conflicts and conflicts of roles are society's concern. Each person is a gestalt of internalized roles, and "conflicts among individuals in a highly developed and organized human society are . . . conflicts among their respective selves . . . each with its definite social structure." This applies as well to conflicts within a person; they are conflicts between various selves within us. Their resolution, according to Mead, requires rethinking the social context and reconstructing the self "by reconstructions of the particular social situations, and modifications of the given framework of social relationships, . . . these reconstructions being performed . . . by the minds of the individuals in whose experiences . . . these conflicts take place."[21]

That a social context and a self are interrelated is also part of my argument. We have seen that the conditions necessary for autonomous and responsible action are narrow, and they are not found everywhere. This was brought home by the way that actions of artificial persons are fractured, and it was further underscored by the anonymity of bureaucratic actions. The conditions for action are crucially connected with the conception of what a

[20] George Herbert Mead, *Mind, Self and Society* (Chicago: University of Chicago Press, 1950), 162, 164.

[21] Ibid., 307–8. Anthropologist James Averill makes a similar point: "Through the process of socialization, aspects of culture are internalized to form parts of an individual's own character structure"; "An Analysis of Psychophysiological Symbolism and Its Influence on Theories of Emotion," *Journal of the Theory of Social Behaviour* 4, 2 (1974): 183–84.

person *is*—what it means to be one—in our culture and in others, and how that concept is embodied in a culture's practices.

Consider our difficulty in understanding the Japanese custom of *ringi*, which diffuses responsibility so that no agent can be identified with a decision and thus both protects individuals and discourages them from taking action on their own. Some say this practice reflects the Japanese tendency to submerge personal identity in the identity of the group, and one psychologist observes that the Japanese have problems being conscious of a self.[22] It is evident in any case that such Japanese institutions and customs are connected somehow with their consciousness of self.

We can assume that a connection between society and self holds for us as well, though the picture from such close range is fuzzier. Let us assume, however, that what it means to be a person in our culture is both reflected in and shaped by our institutions.[23] If the moral worth of an individual is of prime importance, that will show in our institutions; and through their forms and ways of functioning, they will encourage or vitiate the respect people have for one another. Thus they will influence people's conception of themselves. Similarly, the Jalē and Gururumba have a particular idea of self, of an individual's importance and what is possible and permissible, that is palpable in their practices.

The foregoing discussion suggests, however vaguely, a picture of our culture's problems with responsibility. It points to the existence of a deep and intractable conflict between the shape of

[22] L. Takeo Doi, "*Amae*: A Key Concept for Understanding Japanese Personality Structure," in T. S. Lebra and W. P. Lebra, eds., *Japanese Culture and Behavior*, (Honolulu: University of Hawaii Press, 1974), 145–164. In another article, Doi describes the Japanese inclination to identify themselves with their organizations. He writes, "If the rejection of the 'small self' in favor of the 'larger self' is extolled as a virtue, it becomes easier for [the individual] to act in concert with the group"; *The Anatomy of Dependence*, trans. Mark Harbison (Tokyo: Kodansha International, 1962), 135. Another scholar, William Ouichi, puts it more strongly, saying that in the Japanese context, "the most central social value which emerged, the one value without which the society could not continue, was that an individual does not matter"; *Theory Z* (Reading, Mass.: Addison-Wesley, 1981), 65.

[23] Arthur Kuflik criticizes the saying that autonomy is inalienable and argues that a person can abdicate it for various reasons; "The Inalienability of Autonomy," *Philosophy and Public Affairs* 13, 4 (Fall 1984): esp. 284–98. However, Kuflik doesn't focus on the way institutions preempt a person's autonomy.

institutions and the requirements of moral responsibility as we understand them. The conflict is between the demand that we hold people responsible for their actions and the institutional arrangements that muddy both the attribution of responsibility and the exercise of individual choice. Ours is therefore a schizo-phrenic posture, for on the one hand we insist on knowing who did a misdeed; yet at the same time we obscure the determina-tion of who did it.

v

The gist of my argument is this. The ability to speak for others that makes artificial persons both useful and attractive also frus-trates the conditions of responsibility. This fact casts a moral shadow on all such practices and the institutions—the bar, the military, political representatives, corporations—that embody artificial persons. The underlying reasons for difficulty are vari-ous and intractable. One is the comparison of professional roles with those of actors, an analogy that helps insulate the roles from moral criticism. Another is a wrong conception of repre-sentative government, inspired by the idea that government could act *as* the citizens and not need to be distinguished as a peculiar kind of agent. Then there is an emphasis on function-alism that makes moral questions out of bounds in working con-texts. A fourth is that we can use the term "person" for legal purposes to cover whatever entity we please, without concern for the "person" of moral theory, and thus create confusion.

And as we have seen, the resulting problems are also mul-tiple. Perhaps the biggest moral issue is the breakdown of au-tonomy as a feature of human action, and this has consequences of two kinds. First, a person's action fails in a critical way to be *his*, because the phenomenological aspects of the action are sev-ered from his decisions. Second, moral criticism is unable to lo-cate responsibility; thus responsibility-free zones emerge where moral judgments lack purchase. The features of artificial per-sons further entail that we cannot be represented morally, that moral representation in politics and other areas is impossible. For it to be possible, representatives would need to speak and act non-autonomously; but this in turn would vitiate their ac-countability. Thus, although much modern social and political theory assumes that representing others is not only possible, but beneficial and estimable, that view is deeply mistaken.

Despite recommendations from many sides, problems of professional responsibility cannot be dealt with through specialized codes of ethics. For these assume the discreteness of roles and a detachment of roles from non-role life that fosters non-autonomous action. Nor, I argue, can the solution be a calculated revision of the moral vocabulary, with a concomitant change in our moral intuitions. Moral terms have our perceptions linked to them, and words and perceptions both are part of our moral understanding. To change the terms of discussion in order to cast a solution would beg the question. It is also impossible.

Finally, I argue that the concept of person that emphasizes both discretionary action and attribution of responsibility becomes fragile where these aspects are muddied or diffused. In the Japanese context, an individual does not take a central role and exercise her fullest powers of decision making. At the same time, she is protected from the penalties of full responsibility; it would be unsurprising if she is also confused about her distinctness as a person.

A system of institutions and practices can thus alter the way people—*including us*—view themselves. The context in which we act determines whether our dimensions are larger or shrunken and whether our moral stature—our capacity for moral action—is more or less central to our selves. When we accept and live among the ambiguities of artificial persons, when in that ambiguity we despair of locating responsibility, we stand at the edge of a context where these selves are diminished. The time has come to look toward the possibilities for change.

NINE

Making Changes

Our whole life is startlingly moral. There is never an instant's truce be-
tween virtue and vice.   Henry David Thoreau, *Walden*

IT IS POSSIBLE to retain a large measure of moral autonomy
and responsibility in contemporary settings if we are willing to
make radical revisions, both in our ways of thinking and in our
institutions. First, I have argued we should reject the language
of role moralities and dissolve the boundaries between person
and role. A second point is connected with this: that we must be
more aware of how our common metaphors of instrumentality
encourage a calloused and dehumanizing view of persons, how
they can lead to inferences that obstruct a full moral view of the
human creature. For it is that creature who, on the one hand,
deserves respect and, on the other, should be held responsible.
Third, in evaluating institutions, we should consider not only
their usefulness in producing wide social goods but also their
moral effects on individuals in them, particularly the attitudes
they encourage in the name of their defined function. This dimension is neglected when institutions are founded and justified simply on broad, impersonal considerations of public benefit, as Thomas Nagel describes.

   We also need to change our vision of existing agents, to real-
ize, for example, that morally the military is *not* an arm of society, acting in its stead. It is a force with a life of its own, with its
own ways of operating and goals and needs. To project our
ways, our scruples, and our visions onto it is to indulge in a
fantasy. Therefore, when we send it to *act for us*, it must nevertheless act as itself. Similarly, government and its members must
frame their goals and operate through their own means. The

same is true for other artificial persons. Morally speaking, surrogates are impossible, and understanding that would change a
great deal.

I

Concern for the citizen's moral status and well-being is central
in the classical accounts of community and appears in the char-
ters of early American colonies; the community was conceived
as both fulfilling and nourishing the rational human being. Such
"communitarianism" stands in contrast to the atomistic vision
associated with liberal individualism, a vision whose independent, competitive creatures have only their protective self-
interest as a motive to form a community at all. In turn, on this
account, the community needs to serve such self-interests. I
have joined the criticism of this view and argued that it gives too
spare a picture of human lives and too little purchase on the
moral dimension of social issues.[1] However, I am not communitarian to the degree of thinking, as Aristotle does, that a person
can only be viewed as part of a larger whole, that the whole is
"prior to" the individual. One can also view a person in terms of
genetic endowments, as a member of the animal kingdom, as a
cellular structure; a person can be seen in terms of background,
family, and class; or as a type of personality, an exemplary kind
of character, a set of dispositions, even as a type defined by the
horoscope. On my argument, it is not necessary to hold that
man's nature is *essentially* social any more than to hold that it is
essentially physical, or essentially anything. At the same time,
however, *moral* discussion begins with people *in their relations
with one another*, which is to say, in a community or social setting
of some kind. Therefore, our discussion has been necessarily
framed by social contexts.

We have seen that acting with moral autonomy means acting
from one's convictions rather than from external direction; in
turn, such autonomy is the condition for holding a person responsible. Thus, if we want moral responsibility to retain meaning, we need to protect the scope of autonomy from becoming
assimilated, diffused, and lost in the complexities of organiza-

[1]My objections are found in the last chapter of *Equality and the Rights of Women*
(Ithaca, N.Y.: Cornell University Press, 1980) and in the first three chapters of *The
Grammar of Justice* (Ithaca, N.Y.: Cornell University Press, 1987).

tions. Any kind of work will add some obligations to an individual's personal ones, but these need not be incompatible with moral autonomy. They need not preclude a self that recognizes and grapples with the tensions of many responsibilities, a self that grows in understanding from choosing and executing choices, and matures in the course of living in their shadow.

II

The large issues we have raised point to avenues where change would be constructive, where the conditions in which people act would create the implications of responsibility we desire. Such avenues are broad, and do not define particular programs or policies, but they help in the further task of setting such policies.

What general kinds of institutional changes would address some of the problems we raised? There are various options, and we don't need to speak of (correct) solutions to a problem or (right) answers. Most important is that a large opportunity awaits an agile and morally informed imagination.

Consider some fairly specific changes that have been proposed for the legal profession. For instance, David Luban urges that an attorney should be morally active in her role, and leave behind the vision of lawyers as morally neutral, nonjudgmental figures. Luban proposes that "we must ask ourselves which of our ideals would be threatened if lawyers were actively to engage their clients regarding the morality of their projects, and to dissociate themselves from projects that are immoral." His answer is, none. To the objection that lawyers would then be "filters," determining, perhaps idiosyncratically, what projects get forwarded, Luban responds, why not? "To back off from moral activism on the grounds that it is presumptuous to judge the morality of someone else's projects would imply that the lawyer possesses less moral insight than anyone else: it would amount to a plea of diminished moral capacity." Lawyers are preeminently situated and trained to act as moral counselors to their clients, he thinks. "It is not moral activism that is anomalous, but moral nonaccountability."[2]

[2]David Luban, *Lawyers and Justice* (Princeton, N.J.: Princeton University Press, 1989), 171, 161.

Since a lawyer has great discretion about which cases to take
and then how to pursue them, he should use that discretion to
influence his client and enrich his moral understanding, Luban
proposes. Other members of the community exert pressure
against people who act unethically. Why shouldn't lawyers become moral counselors to their clients and try to dissuade those
with morally shady projects? Such counseling would require a
personal relation in which the lawyer is both educator and moral
advisor; it means he no longer functions as an instrument but as
a whole person, whose integrity is on the line and whose credi-
bility depends on things besides his competence in law and usefulness as an instrument.

Why should anyone think a lawyer qualified for this assignment, part priest and part practical advisor? Luban answers that
"legal training with its cultivation of practical judgment should
enable lawyers to form a better picture of the human consequences of institutional arrangements than can those of us who
have no comparable training." The lawyer, he says, "is logician,
scientist, and connoisseur of mankind." He is a specialist in human morality and must accept the obligations that go with that
expertise. His training and experience put a lawyer in a powerful position, both for raising a client's moral consciousness and
for changing the law. "Lawyers have the opportunity to make
the law better by law reform activity and to make their clients
better by using their advisory role to awaken the clients to the
public dimension of their activities, to steer them in the direction of the public good."[3] A lawyer's discretion, like a judge's, is
a powerful force for good. If, despite legal counsel, the client
persists in a morally doubtful project, the lawyer can exercise
"the Lysistratian prerogative" and withhold his services.[4]

In a similar vein, William Simon proposes that attorneys
should "take those actions that . . . seem most likely to promote

---

[3]Ibid., 170–71.

[4]It hardly needs saying that many do not view the function of judges in Luban's way. Anthony Hartle uses the judge's position as a model of a "fully differentiated" role: that is, judges "should adjudicate solely in accordance with the
law, without regard to their own or other moral evaluations. They should judge
in the name of the higher moral ends served by the institution of law"; *Moral
Issues in Military Decision Making* (Lawrence: University Press of Kansas, 1989),
109. The reference on withholding services is to Sophocles' play *Lysistrata*, in
which wives refuse to sleep with their husbands until the men stop the war they
are engaged in.

justice." He calls attention to the fact that judgment is built into the profession because legal arguments "determine the practical meaning of legislative commands. . . . [Thus] the lawyer cannot escape involvement in lawmaking." To give weight to this vision, he observes that in the American tradition "the lawyer has been both an advocate and an 'officer of the court,' with responsibilities to third parties, the public, and the law." There may be tension between these responsibilities, he concedes, but their moral coloring cannot be ignored.[5] Like Luban's, Simon's proposal would radically reshape the profession of the bar.

Are these proposals more severe than is justified? Some would say so. Bernard Williams argues that *everyone* needs to limit his obligations and commitments to others. Each person has some "ground projects" or matters of deepest commitment, and these have priority over other considerations; other things must fit around them, including the public good. "There can come a point at which it is quite unreasonable for a man to give up, in the name of that impartial good ordering of the world of moral agents, something which is a condition of his having any interest in being around in that world at all."[6] What a person deeply cares about comes first and has first claim on his decisions. This means that for someone dedicated to the profession of law, *that* project may define the limits of his other commitments, including some moral ones. Luban's answer would be that a lawyer has a moral commitment to his community *through* being a lawyer and not apart from it. Mature moral judgment is an important quality in lawyers and judges, as it is in military officers; their professions should *join them* to society, not separate them from it.[7] Thus, what it is reasonable for a person to give up has to be illuminated by such inherent moral considerations. It is a persuasive idea.

[5] William Simon, "Ethical Discretion in Lawyering," *Harvard Law Review* 101, 6 (Apr. 1988): 1125, 1133, 1090, 1091.

[6] Bernard Williams, "Persons, Character and Morality," in Amelie Rorty, ed., *The Identities of Persons* (Berkeley: University of California Press, 1976), 210.

[7] Holmes would also say that moral engagement and wide vision are necessary to a lawyer's fullest satisfaction: "Happiness . . . cannot be won simply by being counsel for great corporations and having [a large income]. . . . It is through [the more theoretical] aspects of the law that you not only become a great master in your calling, but connect your subject with the universe and catch an echo of the infinite"; "The Path of the Law," in *Collected Legal Papers* (New York: Harcourt Brace & Co., 1920), 202.

Another and more radical option is to eliminate or discourage the practice of advocacy and require any party to a legal dispute to speak for herself. Gerald Postema briefly considers the possibility of deprofessionalizing law and requiring every person to represent herself; that would indeed eliminate the "social value" of professional advocates with their problematic positions. But he stops short of endorsing this because it would "involve a radical restructuring of the entire legal system."[8] Indeed it would.

Still, self-advocacy was once the policy of ancient Athenians. "Originally, and perhaps always in theory," one scholar says, "the conduct of cases in court was solely the affair of the parties immediately concerned, each of whom was expected to make his plea in person." Only young and inexperienced parties could be represented, and then the representative should be a family member or a close friend. Over time and with the growth in the number of court cases, however, mature people sought help from speakers whose effectiveness was proven, giving work to those who were clever with argument. Citizens even memorized speeches written for them to present in court. But while early advocates claimed friendship or family connection to justify their service, "by the end of the fourth century [B.C.], at least, a body of pleaders existed who formed something like a distinct and recognized profession."[9] This marked the beginning of professional legal advocacy.

All these ways of dealing with legal ethics acknowledge morality's central importance in law. But there is still another connection, Lon Fuller argues. Besides reflecting the moral judgments of a community, law is bound to morality in another way. "When I drive carefully as a good citizen . . . I forget to what extent my conceptions of my duty as a driver have been shaped by the daily activities of the traffic police." The same applies to business conduct: "as business men we may perform our con-

[8] Gerald Postema, "Moral Responsibility in Professional Ethics," *New York University Law Review* 55, 1 (Apr. 1980): 81–82.

[9] J. Walter Jones, *The Law and Legal Theory of the Greeks* (London: Oxford University Press, 1956), 145. Plato's attitude toward such advocates is shown in the *Laws*; xi 937d–938c (cited by Jones, 147). He proposes that a pleader who helped obstruct justice out of professional ambition should be precluded from appearing in court in future, and a second offense should be punishable by death. This accords with Socrates' condemnation of sophists who taught people how to plead an unjust cause as persuasively as a just one.

tracts not because we are afraid of a law suit, but because we feel that it is our duty to do so. But would this same conception of duty exist if the law enforced no contracts . . . ? In the moral environment out of which this conception of duty arises, is not the law itself one of the most important elements?" Morality not only stands behind law, but gains force through the law's presence. Therefore, "the judge in deciding cases is not merely laying down a system of minimum restraints designed to keep the bad man in check, but is in fact helping to create a body of common morality which will define the good man."[10] Law on this view is an inseparable part of the context in which we learn about morality and helps to shape our acceptance of moral standards. That means the profession cannot be morally neutral, it must be engaged somehow.

Some similar conclusions can be drawn about the institutions of government. Undoubtedly, government reflects the values of the community and is in that respect morally charged. At the same time, its officials are expected to provide models of citizenly concern, to serve as examples and guides for the watchful citizenry, much as law guides morality. This function then precludes the justifiability of dirty hands. A representative's position gives him a larger view of the community's welfare, a vantage point for judging the effects of policies on the citizens. Thus, by both his arguments and his actions, he should encourage citizens to put parochial considerations aside and replace them with larger ones, to relinquish short-term advantages for the longer run, including even their distant progeny. On this vision, government's job is, in part, moral leadership and education.[11] Therefore, a representative's willingness to give moral

[10] Lon L. Fuller, *The Law in Quest of Itself* (Chicago: The Foundation Press, 1978), 136, 137. Fuller further underscores the unity of morals and law: "If we look to those rules of morality which have enough teeth in them to act as serious deterrents to men's pursuit of their selfish interests, we will find that far from being 'extra-legal' they are intimately and organically connected with the functionings of the legal order"; 136.

[11] The idea that the state should contribute to the moral character of the citizens is traceable to the ancient Greeks. It is also found in early constitutions of some American colonies, of Massachusetts for instance. A contrasting view is stated by Holmes in "The Path of the Law"; he argues that a sharp separation between law and morality is essential to a clear view of the law. However, this does not prevent him from acknowledging that "the law is the witness and external deposit of our moral life . . . [and] the practice of it . . . tends to make good citizens and good men"; 110. His position thus appears to be inconsistent.

leadership and his possession of a good character might be primary qualifications for the job.

This picture is formed by acknowledging the moral connection of government to citizens and by letting that connection help to shape a representative's duties. Constituents, on their side, would need to understand that their representative is not sent to perform a job for them; they must see him as, in part, helping them understand the community's needs and how they can undertake, jointly with him, to meet them.[12] But at the same time he needs to be the responsive student of citizens; only in that way can he succeed in his tasks.[13] Neither aspect resembles the conception of an uncritical instrument of others' purposes.

Many of our government representatives see their responsibilities in something like this way; they struggle to connect their own vision of what needs to be done with that of the citizens, to communicate and persuade, and also to listen, to strive to understand their constituents' views and deal with them honestly. But described in this way, an electee's job no longer sounds much like representation—or it is representation in an altered sense. It may better be likened to the work of a doctor, who both decides for and consults with her patient, always keeping in focus the patient's overall welfare.

Accepting this picture of the relation of government to citizens means, first of all, a change from the traditional conception of representation, the conception that incorporates Hobbes's artificial person. Theorists and voters alike need to revise their ideas about this relation, and from that new understanding some concrete changes would follow directly. For instance, we would see in an unforgiving light how pernicious lobbies and special interest groups are. That is, they interfere with the rightful job of government professionals,which is to concern themselves always with the community and its welfare, and with its understanding of itself.

[12] Nancy Schwartz, in *The Blue Guitar* (Chicago: University of Chicago Press, 1988), criticizes the traditional theory of representation as a "transmission belt" conception where the citizens' private interests are expected to guide their representatives.

[13] This echoes, against a different background, the tension described by Hanna Pitkin: "The representative must act in such a way that, although he is independent . . . no conflict arises between them"; see Chapter 6, section III, above.

III

Corporations also pose an obvious and fruitful target for change, partly because of their ubiquity and partly because of the great numbers of people who participate in them. Here, as with government, theory is a poor guide to assessing moral implications and to planning changes. The single-function conception of a corporation promotes a certain atmosphere and structure. That is, the specialized corporate function leads to specialization within it and to the detachment of role obligations from morals. Thus, the first task is to see the corporation in a way that makes it accessible to moral criticism; that means seeing it as a collection of human beings working together.

People combine their efforts in different ways, and cooperative efforts can take different forms. In families, members with various goals and ideas coordinate and adjust their activities to one another: a car is used by one person one night, its use by another deferred; everyone contributes to shopping lists; and so on. Command and obedience don't determine how the members associate with one another; instead respect for the bonds of personal obligation are central. Most committees and many boards work in a similar way insofar as they are viewed as associations of people; some jobs are separated but many are shared, and cooperation takes different forms at different times.

But it will be protested that a large corporation really depends on more stylized action, where everyone plays his part within a synchronized plan and puts aside his initiative if it might interfere. The artificial person fits into this picture neatly, as we have seen: the corporation acts selflessly as the non-human agent of others, and within it, individual interests are likewise subordinated to the whole. In both frameworks, corporate actions have moral neutrality.

What is wrong with this picture is that any organization of people is necessarily a setting where moral qualities and moral relations are endemic. Defining a corporation functionally does not dispose of this fact. Thus, a better conception would be that it is a collection of people, with all their human dimensions, engaged in working together. With such a theoretical basis, arrangements could be compared and evaluated in terms of these dimensions and the human values they entail. Suppressing and neglecting them for the sake of efficiency would not be plausible.

Whatever form such revisions took, several features seem to be indicated by the problems we have discussed: there would be more emphasis on individual decisions, and clear responsibility for them; in that context, the idea that one person can be responsible—morally responsible—for the work of others would seem foolish. More real authority would belong to people who do the productive work of a corporation, not removed to a higher level; and this in turn means involving many more productive people in the overall coordination of projects. The net result would be a drastic decrease in bureaucratic and corporate structures, a more horizontal and less vertical form of organization. And such revised arrangements would eliminate the requirement that people leave the moral aspects of their beings at the door.

IV

Supposing that corporate structures might be changed in this direction, could such changes apply to the military? That seems doubtful; the military surely *does* have a single function, and considerations of autonomy and respect have no legitimate place in it. A vertical organization, a strict line authority, is the only appropriate form of organization for it. But this objection is hasty. First, the army is composed of citizens, and therefore a claim for autonomy exists even here. But more crucially, the consequences of army training on a person's character are important even—and perhaps *especially*—in wartime. Military personnel call for the same concern as other citizens do; they are not pawns of the community.

Adm. James Stockdale, war hero and prisoner in Vietnam, has repeatedly expressed concern about the characteristics the military needs in its personnel. He describes a type of early American, which he sees as typified by Benjamin Franklin: "They were do-it-yourself guys: self-reliant, strong-willed, cautious, suspicious. . . . They liked to make up their own minds. . . . [They] were men of conscience." These were people to be trusted, he thinks, who act on their own judgment, who take initiative and responsibility. Early business leaders, while less individualistic, were somewhat similar: Stockdale cites Carnegie as a leader who was concerned about those who worked with and for him. But as businesses grew to giant size, such figures "were gradually displaced by the smoother organization men . . . [who] were more motivated by a fear of failure." And more recently, he argues, these have been replaced by modern gamesmen, "cool, intellectual types, walking calculating machines." What the military needs, he proposes, is people of the "early" type, people of character and independence and humanity. Stockdale associates good military leadership with strong character, sympathy for one's fellows, respect for others, and acknowledgment of responsibility. One's actions show one's mettle: "a person is the sum of his deeds." [14] Since such qualities are needed and need to be developed in the military, there must be opportunities to make individual choices, not simply carry out the decisions of others. But making decisions individually entails the perennial hazard of making the wrong decisions, possibly losing synchronization with others. Stockdale would argue that the risk needs to be taken.

Stockdale's vision of the military relates closely to the issues I have considered, of the connections between autonomy, responsibility, and fractured action. His idealized early American figures identified themselves with their work, set their own standards, and were self-critical. They acted with autonomy, and we are neither tempted to speak of their "roles" nor concerned about any displacement of responsibility. Nevertheless, the possibility of such action seems unrealistic, given the gigantic size of modern military forces. The practical problems would be overwhelming: with such severe organizational changes would large-scale coordination any longer be possible? Stockdale seems to support a compromise change that would accommodate the Carnegie type of officer, one who maintains his standards despite the large organization and remains morally sensitive to his relations and obligations to others. But even such a compromise view of the military is radical and would require sweeping changes.

Others besides Stockdale have found difficulties in the orga-

[14] James Stockdale, *A Vietnam Experience* (Stanford, Calif.: Hoover Press, 1984), 138–40, 121. He adds that not only the military needs such people: "Throughout our society, we need people . . . who are . . . imaginative, educated, and eager to handle the unexpected."

nizational size and complexity of military organizations. As W. B. Gallie writes, Tolstoy held it a "primary truth of war . . . that in war the most intelligible units are relatively small groups of men, in close physical contact and operationally independent, who share . . . the same reactions and feelings."[15] Personal contact, small size, and independence are the chief factors to emphasize in forming contexts that will allow more individual decision. Only in such a changed context can a military person be held morally responsible for what he does, and only in such a context does the concept of "war criminal" make much sense.

v

Altering a multitude of historic institutions is a formidable project. In the end we, like the Athenians, may insist that agents are indispensable for commerce and that changing such arrangements would too greatly upset the buying and selling on which the community depends. And theorists of government and corporations may see change as too hazardous to justify the benefits. The motive for tackling these gargantuan projects of reform, however, is that the alternative is a further thinning in the meaning of responsibility, and the chronic inconsistency of demanding responsibility on one side while nurturing institutions that defeat it on the other. A decision to change is acutely a moral decision, and moral courage is needed to make it.

To move toward such changes we need only one simple, governing principle: that is, to strive to create the conditions required by the moral paradigm. Those conditions are the ones that allow people to make their own decisions, not from some abstract rational vantage point, but from within the context of their many relations and obligations to others, a context where they are responsible on many sides for what they do. In such a setting, professional and corporate obligations exist side by side with a person's other obligations and make their claims in the same moral arena. In it a person works out her decisions, always in her own name; she doesn't lack ground for rejecting morally doubtful projects; and she has full responsibility for both her decisions and her acts.

[15] W. B. Gallie, *Philosophers of Peace and War* (London: Cambridge University Press, 1978), 104.

In this picture there clearly cannot be artificial persons in Hobbes's sense. There cannot be people who act, but not as themselves, and no superfigures whose agents extend and enlarge their capacities. The goal of this strategy is to reclaim and make palpable the conception of self that moral theory shows us, one whose actions are both critical and creative with respect to obligations, and whose moral convictions take visible, individualized forms.

A responsible person exists only against a certain kind of background and in some contexts will disappear, but in the right background his moral dimensions and importance are enhanced. Besides our desire for locating responsibility when misdeeds occur, our commitment to an individual's moral importance and our respect for moral autonomy provide powerful motives for making institutional changes, and they suggest how to make them. Improvement admits of degrees; we can approach the paradigm by more or less, capturing more or less individual responsibility. What we can not do is think our way to greater individual responsibility, or consistently demand it, while changing nothing.

Index

In this index "f" after a number indicates a separate reference on the next page, and "ff" indicates separate references on the next two pages. A continuous discussion over two or more pages is indicated by a span of numbers. *Passim* is used for a cluster of references in close but not consecutive sequence.

Library of Congress Cataloging-in-Publication Data

Wolgast, Elizabeth Hankins
    Ethics of an artificial person: lost responsibility in
professions and organizations—Elizabeth Wolgast.
      p. cm.
    Includes index.
    ISBN 0-8047-2034-7 (alk. paper):
      1. Juristic persons—Moral and ethical aspects. 2. Professional
ethics. 3. Juristic persons—United States—Moral and ethical
aspects. 4. Professional ethics—United States. I. Title.
K650.W65 1992
346.01'3—dc20
[342.613]   91-42508
                                             CIP

⊝ This book is printed on acid-free paper